SAVOR SM

The Royal Caribbean International Cookbook

Volume 3

Dear Guest,

Welcome to our 3rd edition of *Savor*[sm], Royal Caribbean International's tribute to the culinary arts and talent throughout our fleet. Due to popular demand, we have extended our recipes in *Savor* into this new and improved version. We have also taken the suggestions of our readers to add new features to our book such as new wine pairings, degree of difficulties and the addition of the metric system.

Savor invites you to sail with us as we take you on a culinary journey like no other. Our team of esteemed chefs from around the globe will help you navigate your kitchen to create meals that make your taste buds dance and inspire your culinary creativity!

Savor features our guests' favorite recipes from the Royal Caribbean International fleet and our innovative menus onboard. This book reflects the dedication, creativity and professionalism of our Executive Chefs and Food & Beverage Teams. The fabulous dishes and fan-fare you have enjoyed while sailing with us are now at your fingertips!

You will meet our chefs and their own personal favorite recipes. This book also features tips, interesting culinary facts and history, wine pairings and enticing cocktails.

We invite you to sample the dishes and recipes during your cruise, not only in our main dining rooms, but also in our internationally acclaimed specialty restaurants, Chops and Portofino. Cocktails and coffees can be found in our popular bar venues such as Vintages, Café Promenade, Café Latte-tudes, Boleros and our long-time favorite Champagne Bar.

In addition to all that, if you're lucky, the Executive Chefs featured in this book may be onboard your cruise. Seek them out and have your book signed. It's a great opportunity to chat and get some unique and fascinating insight on what happens behind the scenes when producing 15,000 meals per day with fresh, natural ingredients. Did you know that we bake all our breads, produce all cakes and desserts and create new pieces of art out of fruit, ice & chocolate daily, right on board? Were you aware of the fact that our chefs and cooks hail from over 50 countries, making ours the most diverse infusion of international culinary talent on or off the seven seas?

Don't forget to bring back your *Savor*[sm] cookbook on your next cruise, to have it autographed by as many of our chefs as possible, to make it your very own special edition, enhancing its personal and unique value.

Whether re-creating one of our magnificent Chef's Signature dishes or indulging in one of our delectable desserts, this book will get you cooking like a world class chef! We have a world of talent to share, so let the adventure begin in your kitchen and continue on your next Royal Caribbean International Cruise!

Bon Voyage and Bon Appétit!

Frank Weber

Frank Weber
Vice President, Food & Beverage Operations
Royal Caribbean International

SAVOR℠

The Royal Caribbean International Cookbook

Volume 3

It is my pleasure to welcome you to *Savor℠ Volume 3*, a cookbook created to celebrate our chefs' talent and creativity.

May it be for a romantic dinner or a party with a friend, *Savor* recipes have been designed with home cooking in mind. Easy to create but deliciously gourmet, they will transport you back onboard our beautiful ships and allow you to relive your special cruise memories.

I would like to add that $1.00 of your cookbook purchase will benefit the Make-A-Wish® Foundation and its noble mission to 'share the power of a wish' with children who have life-threatening medical conditions.

Since 2000, Royal Caribbean International has been a national partner of the Make-A-Wish® Foundation and has helped more than 1,138 children with cruise wishes come true, through the Wishes at Sea program.

Founded in 1980, after a little boy named Chris Greicus realized his heartfelt wish to become a police officer, the Make-A-Wish® Foundation has blossomed into a worldwide phenomenon, reaching more than 174,000 children around the world.

In addition, we have instituted the Walk for Wishes® program, which encourages our guests to take daily walks with our officers and staff while onboard their cruise, with all the profits going to Make-A-Wish®.

As a valued guest of Royal Caribbean International, we appreciate you sailing with us and your contribution to Make-A-Wish®.

Lisa Bauer

Lisa Bauer
Senior Vice President
Hotel Operations
Royal Caribbean International

Wines That Hit Just the Right Note

One of the pleasures of cooking fine cuisine is choosing a wine to enhance your meal. As in musical composition, sometimes you may want sweet harmony between the main elements; other times you may want a bold contrast for drama. You are the maestro. So how do you choose?

Wine is as important to fine dining as the meal itself...wine does actually make food taste better. The acidity present in wines awakens the taste buds, unlocking flavors so that the full range can be enjoyed. This doesn't mean more acidity is better; it's all about the balance between the food and the wine. Classic pairings such as shellfish with a buttery Chardonnay, or beef and big red wines always work, but don't be afraid to experiment and find your own favorites.

Consider the texture, feel, aromas and flavors of the food and wine... pair robust wines with rich, hearty foods and light, refreshing wines with delicate foods. Or go for drama...a high-acidity wine like Sauvignon Blanc can unleash even more creamy flavor from a dish like pasta Alfredo. Don't worry about one "right" choice, there are as many choices as there are chefs...and hungry guests.

Naturally, our chefs have their own opinions! We've included some of their suggestions on wine pairings to get you started on composing with confidence. Look for the wine glass throughout the book for the chef's own recommendation. Enjoy!

Vintages Lounge | *Freedom of the Sea*

"A good meal is wholeness, when everything gels. I like it when everything complements each other, including the wines. That's the way we look at performance—it's the contribution to the whole."

— Ramsey Lewis, American jazz musician

Table of Contents

These icons give a rating system for the degree of difficulty in making the recipes in this cookbook.
1= Easiest   5=Most Difficult

♛♛♛♛♛ = 1   ♛♛♛♛♛ = 2   ♛♛♛♛♛ = 3   ♛♛♛♛♛ = 4   ♛♛♛♛♛ = 5

Salads

*1 pound (450 g) fresh Alaskan salmon fillet,
skin off, trimmed*

MARINADE
*1 tablespoon (15 g) anise seeds
1 tablespoon (15 g) coriander seeds
1 tablespoon (15 g) juniper berries
1 tablespoon (15 g) white peppercorn
2 tablespoons (30 g) lemon zest
3 tablespoons (45 g) orange zest
2 tablespoons (30 g) peeled and grated ginger
1/2 cup (115 g) sugar
1/4 cup (60 g) salt*

DRESSING
*1 white onion, finely chopped
1 teaspoon (5 ml) vegetable oil
3/4 cup (175 ml) soy sauce
2 tablespoons (30 ml) corn oil
2 tablespoons (30 ml) sesame oil
2 tablespoons (30 ml) rice vinegar
Juice of 1/2 orange
1 teaspoon (5 g) sugar
1 teaspoon (5 g) mustard
Salt and freshly ground black pepper*

SALAD MIX
3 cups (700 g) organic mesclun mix

GARNISH
*4 pansies
1/4 bunch chervil
1/4 bunch opal basil
1/4 bunch chives*

CITRUS FRAGRANCED ALASKAN SALMON
WITH ORGANIC FIELD GREENS

For marinade, crush anise seeds, coriander, juniper berries and pepper in a mortar, add citrus zests, ginger, sugar and salt and mix well.

Arrange a large piece of plastic wrap onto a working surface and sprinkle it with half of spice mixture. Lay salmon fillet on top and sprinkle with remaining spice mixture. Wrap tightly into the plastic wrap and refrigerate for 20 hours.

For dressing, over medium heat in a small sauté pan, heat vegetable oil and sauté onion for 3 minutes, until translucent. Transfer to a blender, add remaining ingredients and blend until very fine. Cover and refrigerate.

Toss mesclun with 1/2 of the dressing and slice salmon into 2 inch (5 cm) strips.

To serve, place mesclun on chilled plates and arrange salmon around, drizzle with remaining dressing and garnish with pansies and fresh herbs.

Cooking should be a carefully balanced

reflection of all the good things in life.

To cultivate a passion for the very best

you must commit to prepare and serve

only the very best. Every cruise gives us

the freedom to tantalize your taste buds.

Josef Jungwirth

Josef Jungwirth,
Director, Culinary Operations, CEC, CCA

Chef Josef joined Royal Caribbean International in March 1999 as Corporate Executive Chef. Josef was born in Koeingwiesen, Austria. At 15, he began a 4-year apprenticeship at Hotel zur Post in St. Valentin, Austria, followed by working as Chef Saucier on Cunard's QE2. He has held numerous positions with Cunard, as well as working in some of the finest restaurants and hotel kitchens in Europe and the United States. Josef also enjoyed a stint with Hyatt International at the Grand Hyatt in Seoul, Korea. Josef is a Master Chef and member of many professional organizations, including the Chaîne des Rôtisseurs and was awarded the "Culinary Order of Merit" from the World Master Chef's Society.

CROUTONS

4 tablespoons (60 ml) extra virgin olive oil
1 cup (250 g) sourdough bread, cubed
Salt and freshly ground black pepper

INGREDIENTS

3 heads romaine lettuce, washed, dried
and cut lengthwise
1/4 cup (60 g) shaved Parmesan cheese

DRESSING

3 cloves garlic
3 tablespoons (45 ml) freshly squeezed lemon juice
5 anchovy fillets, drained or
2 teaspoons (10 g) anchovy paste
2 teaspoons (10 g) Dijon mustard
2 teaspoons (10 ml) Worcestershire sauce
2 egg yolks
1 cup (240 ml) extra virgin olive oil
Salt

TRADITIONAL CAESAR SALAD

Preheat oven to 380°F or 195°C.

To prepare croutons, place bread on a baking sheet and drizzle with olive oil. Toss well to coat evenly. Season to taste with salt and black pepper. Bake for 10 minutes or until crisp and golden brown. Set aside to cool on a paper towel.

To prepare Caesar dressing, combine all ingredients except oil in a blender or food processor. Blend until smooth. While processing, slowly add oil. Adjust seasoning, cover and refrigerate.

Place romaine hearts on chilled plates, drizzle with Caesar dressing and garnish with Parmesan shavings and croutons. Serve immediately.

Serves 6.

CULINARY NOTES:

Contrary to popular belief, Caesar Salad is not named after Julius Caesar, the famed leader of the Roman Empire, but for Chef Caesar Cardoni, famed Italian restaurateur, who created the dish in Tijuana, Mexico in 1924. The original dish called for coddled whole eggs.

BASIL OIL

1 cup (250 g) firmly packed fresh basil leaves
½ cup (120 ml) extra virgin olive oil
Salt and freshly ground black pepper to taste

INGREDIENTS

1 pound (450 g) red grape tomatoes,
cut in half if large
1⅓ cups (350 g) fresh mozzarella bocconcini
2 tablespoons (30 g) julienned basil
2 tablespoons (30 ml) extra virgin olive oil
Salt and freshly ground black pepper

GARNISH

1½ cups (350 g) mesclun mix
Basil leaves
12 edible flowers (optional)

INSALATA CAPRESE

Grape Tomatoes and Baby Mozzarella Salad

Prepare basil oil by blanching basil in a pan of boiling water for 10 seconds. Drain and rinse with cold water. Pat dry with paper towels and transfer to a blender. Add the oil and purée until smooth. Transfer to a small bowl. Season with salt and black pepper. Cover and refrigerate.

Let stand at room temperature for 30 minutes before using.

In a stainless steel bowl mix grape tomatoes, mozzarella, basil and olive oil. Season with salt and pepper.

Place equal amount of tomatoes and mozzarella in each serving dish.

Garnish with mesclun mix drizzled with basil oil.

Finish with basil leaves and flowers.

Serves 6.

CULINARY NOTES:

Mesclun is also called Spring Mix or Field Greens and is a classic French salad mixture. It is usually made up of young greens and shoots, both wild and cultivated. Radicchio, endive, mâche, frisée, dandelion greens and lollo rosso are often used.

CARPACCIO

$1/2$ pound (250 g) dolphin fish or mahi mahi,
skinned and boneless
$1/2$ pound (250 g) salmon, skinned and boneless
$1/2$ pound (250 g) sea scallops
$1/2$ pound (250 g) tuna, skinned and boneless

MARINADE

1 star anise
$1/4$ teaspoon (1.2 g) cinnamon
$1/4$ teaspoon (1.2 g) nutmeg
$1/4$ teaspoon (1.2 g) allspice
1 teaspoon (5 g) tamarind sauce
1 teaspoon (5 ml) white or dark Jamaican rum
2 tablespoons (30 ml) extra virgin olive oil
Juice of 3 limes
Salt and freshly ground black pepper

SALAD

2 ripe mangoes, peeled and julienned
$1/2$ ripe papaya, peeled and julienned
$1/2$ teaspoon (2.5 g) chopped jalapeño
$1/2$ small red onion, finely chopped
3 tablespoons (45 g) chopped cilantro
1 teaspoon (5 g) peeled and grated ginger
2 teaspoons (10 g) brown sugar
Juice of 1 lime
Juice of 1 orange

GARNISH

$1/4$ bunch cilantro, finely chopped
Freshly ground black pepper

MONTEGO BAY CARPACCIO WITH PAPAYA MANGO SALAD

Samuel Boyd, Executive Chef, CEC

"Chef Sammy", as his colleagues refer to him, comes to us from Montego Bay, Jamaica. Growing up, he was fortunate enough to have excellent schooling enabling him to follow his career choice. He studied at the School of Culinary Arts of Jamaica and graduated at the top of his class. He began his career as an apprentice at the Sandals Royal Caribbean Hotel in Jamaica. In 1989 Samuel joined Commodore Cruise Line's Enchanted Isle where he was promoted to Executive Chef. In 1996 he arrived at Royal Caribbean International where he worked as a Sous Chef and Chef de Cuisine before resuming the position of Executive Chef. During his spare time Samuel enjoys diving and fishing.

Cut fish and scallops in thin slices and arrange on a large plate.

For marinade, mash anise with a mortar and pestle. Combine anise and remaining ingredients in a bowl and mix well. Adjust seasoning with salt and pepper.

Lightly brush marinade over each piece of fish, cover and refrigerate for 2 hours.

For salad, mix mangoes and papaya in a bowl with all ingredients. Cover and refrigerate for 1 hour.

On chilled plates, place a small mound of salad in the center, top with carpaccio and garnish with cilantro. Grind black pepper over plates.

Serves 6.

CHARMOULA MARINADE

1/4 cup (60 ml) extra virgin olive oil
1 small red onion, finely chopped
2 cloves garlic, crushed
1/4 teaspoon (1.2 g) peeled and minced ginger
1/4 teaspoon (1.2 g) cumin
1/4 teaspoon (1.2 g) paprika
1/4 teaspoon (1.2 g) chopped coriander
Pinch cayenne pepper
1 teaspoon (5 g) lemon zest
1 teaspoon (5 g) lime zest
1 teaspoon (5 g) orange zest
1 tablespoon (15 g) chopped parsley
1 tablespoon (15 g) chopped rosemary
Juice of 1/2 lemon
Juice of 1/2 lime
Juice of 1/2 orange
2 tablespoons (30 g) honey
Salt and pepper

2 lamb tenderloins, well-trimmed
2 tablespoons (30 ml) extra virgin olive oil

PEPERONATA

3 tablespoons (45 ml) extra virgin olive oil
3 cloves garlic, crushed
1 red onion cut into strips
1 red bell pepper cut into strips
1 yellow bell pepper, cut into strips
3 Roma tomatoes, peeled, seeded and
cut into strips
1 tablespoon (15 g) chopped rosemary
1 tablespoon (15 g) chopped thyme
Salt and freshly ground black pepper

VINAIGRETTE

1/4 cup (60 ml) rice wine vinegar
2 tablespoons (30 g) chopped mint
1/4 teaspoon (1.2 g) peeled and minced ginger
1/2 tablespoon (7.5 g) honey
1/2 cup (120 ml) vegetable oil
Salt and freshly ground black pepper

1 pound (450 g) mesclun mix

OCEANIC LAMB TENDERLOIN SALAD

For marinade, heat oil and sauté onion, garlic and ginger for 2 minutes, or until fragrant, in a small saucepan over low heat. Do not brown. Add spices, citrus zests and herbs and stir well. Remove from heat and let cool. Transfer mixture to a blender. Add citrus juices and honey. Blend for 2 minutes, until very smooth. Adjust seasoning with salt and pepper. Coat tenderloins with marinade, cover and refrigerate for 3 hours.

For peperonata, over medium heat in a sauté pan, heat oil and sauté garlic until fragrant. Do not brown. Add vegetables and sauté for 5 minutes. Stir in herbs and adjust seasoning. Transfer into a non-reactive bowl, cover and refrigerate.

Preheat oven to 300°F or 150°C.

Heat a skillet over high heat. Add oil and reduce heat to medium. Remove lamb from the marinade, shake off excess liquid and sear medallions on all sides for 5 minutes, until nicely browned. Place on a baking sheet and roast in oven for 5 to 7 minutes or until medium pink. Remove from oven and let rest for 10 minutes. Cover and refrigerate for 2 hours.

For vinaigrette, place vinegar, mint, ginger and honey in a blender. Blend over medium-high speed for 2 minutes, until smooth. Reduce speed and drizzle oil in, a little at a time. Season with salt and pepper and set aside.

Carve lamb into 1/4-inch-thick slices (or 0.6 cm).

Toss mesclun with half of the dressing.

To serve, place mesclun on chilled plates and arrange lamb on top. Garnish with peperonata and drizzle with remaining dressing.

Serves 4.

Peter Howell, Executive Chef, CEC

Chef Peter joined Royal Caribbean International in August 2003. Peter was born in Toowoomba, Australia and raised in Asia. He traveled the world and came back to Australia to pursue a culinary apprenticeship, working in several establishments over 3 years and attending COTAH College of Hospitality. He has more than 27 years of hospitality industry experience in Australia, London and Hong Kong with such companies as the Park Royal Group Australia, the Sheraton and Hilton Hotels, the prestigious Savoy Hotel in London and Hamilton Island Resort in the Whitsundays in Queensland, Australia. Peter enjoys getting out his 5.3 meter boat and going cruising with his wife and six children.

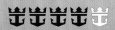

BALSAMIC SYRUP

2 tablespoons (30 ml) extra virgin olive oil
2 shallots, minced
1/2 cup (120 ml) balsamic vinegar

DRESSING

1/2 cup (120 ml) extra virgin olive oil
2 tablespoons (30 ml) sherry
1 tablespoon (15 g) honey
1/3 cup (90 ml) balsamic vinegar
Salt and freshly ground black
pepper to taste

INGREDIENTS

3 pears
Juice of one lemon
1/3 cup (85 g) walnuts
3 tablespoons (45 g) powdered sugar
1/2 cup (120 ml) vegetable oil
4 cups (920 g) mesclun mix
1 (4-ounce) (120 g) slice gorgonzola cheese,
cut into small cubes

PEAR AND GORGONZOLA SALAD

For balsamic syrup, warm olive oil in a sauté pan over medium heat and sauté shallots until translucent. Add balsamic vinegar and reduce to a syrup consistency.

For dressing, place olive oil, sherry, honey and balsamic vinegar in a blender. Season to taste and blend until smooth and emulsified. Allow to rest.

Slice pears lengthwise, remove core and sprinkle with lemon juice.

Spray walnuts with water, then toss in sugar. In a small frying pan, heat oil over high heat and fry walnuts for 2 minutes. Drain and place on paper towels.

In a bowl, mix mesclun with 1/4 of the dressing. Toss well.

On chilled plates, arrange the mesclun, sliced pears, cheese and top with walnuts. Drizzle with balsamic syrup.

Serves 6.

CULINARY NOTES:

Place the gorgonzola in the freezer for 10 minutes prior to cutting. It will be easier and less messy to cube.

Balsamic vinegar is not made with balsam, but is a reference to the fact that it is thick and syrupy. The process of making balsamic vinegar starts by boiling unfermented grape juice to concentrate the flavors. The extract then has Mother of Vinegar added to it and the fermentation process begins. (Mother of Vinegar contains yeasts and Acetobacter bacteria. These bacteria convert the alcohol and sugar into acetic acid or "vinegar.")

The vinegar is then aged for at least 12 years in a series of barrels made from various types of wood including oak, chestnut, mulberry and juniper.

EGGPLANT

1 medium size eggplant, cut into thin slices
1/4 cup (60 ml) extra virgin olive oil
Salt and freshly ground black pepper

MARINARA SAUCE

2 tablespoons (30 ml) extra virgin olive oil
1 large white onion, diced
1 clove garlic
6 ripe tomatoes, peeled, seeded and diced
1/2 teaspoon (2.5 g) chopped oregano
1/2 teaspoon (2.5 g) chopped basil
Salt and freshly ground black pepper

CARROT SALAD

1/4 cup (60 ml) white wine vinegar
3 tablespoons (45 g) sugar
6 medium carrots, peeled and shredded
1/4 cup (60 g) raisins
Salt and freshly grated white pepper

SPICE RUB

1 teaspoon (5 g) cumin
1/2 teaspoon (2.5 g) ground cloves
1 teaspoon (5 g) five spice mix
1 teaspoon (5 g) kosher salt

CHICKEN

6 chicken breasts, boneless and skinless

SALAD

5-ounce (141 g) arugula salad
1 medium red onion, thinly sliced
8-ounce (226 g) fresh green beans, blanched
15 grape tomatoes, sliced lengthwise

DRESSING

1/3 cup (90 ml) sour cream
Juice of 2 lemons
Salt and freshly ground black pepper

GARNISH

Cilantro sprigs
Pappadam, store bought

MOROCCAN SPICED CHICKEN SALAD

Preheat oven to 375°F or 205°C.

For eggplant, grease a grill pan and heat to medium high. Place eggplant slices in the pan, marking each side with grill marks.

Place eggplants into a small sheet pan, season with salt and pepper and drizzle with olive oil. Cover and refrigerate.

For marinara, in a small saucepan over medium heat, warm oil and sauté onion for 4 minutes or until translucent. Add garlic and sauté, stirring constantly. Do not brown.

Add tomatoes and herbs and season with salt and pepper. Cover and simmer for 10 minutes. Set aside.

In a small stainless steel bowl, mix all ingredients for carrot salad. Cover and refrigerate.

In a small stainless steel bowl, mix all ingredients for the spice rub.

Brush chicken with marinara sauce and press with spice rub. Place chicken on a lightly oiled baking sheet and bake in the oven for 20 minutes.

Let cool and cut at an angle.

Finish salad by tossing together the carrot mixture, green beans, onion and tomatoes.

On chilled salad plates, place an eggplant slice and top with carrot mixture and arugula, crown with chicken slices and drizzle with sour cream dressing.

Garnish with cilantro sprigs and serve with a crispy pappadam.

Serves 6.

CULINARY NOTES:

Pappadam (or paapad, pappadum, popadam), thin and crispy Indian wafers, are made by mixing lentil, chickpea or rice flour with salt and peanut oil to make a dough. Seasonings can include chili, cumin, garlic, pepper, etc. The dough is shaped into a round, flat bread and dried in the sun. They can be cooked by deep-frying, baking, roasting over an open flame or microwaving. They can be purchased in most international supermarkets or your local Indian Market.

Alfred Hauser, Executive Chef, CEC

Chef Alfred is a proud member of the Chaîne des Rôtisseurs, a gastronomy society dedicated to the celebration of professionals in the culinary industry. He is also a Certified Executive Chef of the American Culinary Federation. Alfred has been a chef since 1976 and has worked in numerous 5-star hotels and restaurants around the world. He came to work for Royal Caribbean International in 1995 and now oversees more than 100 culinary team members and the preparation of nearly ten thousand meals a day. Alfred's hobbies include going to the movies, rollerblading, reading and playing soccer.

TARTARE
4 ripe avocados, peeled and diced
1 pound medium sized, cooked shrimp, peeled and deveined, diced
2 tablespoons chopped cilantro
2 teaspoons chopped jalapeño
1 shallot, finely chopped
Juice of 2 lemons

TOMATO COULIS
4 large tomatoes
1 tablespoon extra virgin olive oil
Salt and freshly ground black pepper

YOGURT
$1^1/2$ cups plain yogurt
Juice of $1/2$ lemon

GARNISH
6 teaspoons caviar
$1/4$ bunch cilantro
8 cherry tomatoes, halved

AVOCADO AND SHRIMP TARTARE

In a large stainless steel bowl, combine avocado, shrimp, cilantro, jalapeño, shallot and lemon juice. Gently mix. Season with salt and pepper and refrigerate for 2 hours.

For tomato coulis, fill a small pan with water and bring to a boil. Using a sharp knife, gently tear the skin of the tomatoes lengthwise in a couple of spots and place in boiling water for about 3 minutes. Place tomatoes into ice water for 2 minutes or until skin starts to separate from tomato. Peel, cut in half and seed using a small spoon. Transfer tomatoes to a food processor and blend until smooth. Place purée in a bowl, mix in olive oil, salt and pepper. Transfer to a non-reactive bowl, cover and refrigerate 45 minutes, stirring occasionally, until any air bubbles have burst.

On chilled plates, mound avocado mixture into a 3-inch wide by $1/2$-inch high ring mold. Level the mixture and smooth the top. Carefully remove the mold.

Fill a small piping bag with tomato coulis.

Pipe a small border approximately 2 inches (1 cm) from the mold.

Mix yogurt with lemon juice and season with salt and ground pepper. Pipe yogurt mixture inside tomato coulis border to create a contrast in color. Top tartare with caviar. Garnish with cilantro and cherry tomatoes.

Serves 4.

PIZZA DOUGH

2½ teaspoons (1 packet) active dry yeast
1 cup (250 ml) warm water
1 teaspoon (5 g) honey
1 tablespoon (15 ml) extra virgin olive oil
3 cups (700 g) all purpose flour
1 teaspoon (5 g) salt

2 tablespoons (30 ml) extra virgin olive oil

RED ONION JAM

2 tablespoons (30 ml) extra virgin olive oil
1 tablespoon (15 g) butter
10 red onions, peeled and sliced
⅓ cup (60 g) brown sugar
⅓ cup (90 ml) red wine vinegar
Salt and freshly ground black pepper

DUCK CONFIT

2 duck legs confit, purchased

2 cups (500 g) grated mozzarella cheese
2 cups (500 g) grated Fontina cheese
¼ cup (60 g) grated Parmesan cheese
1 teaspoon (5 g) finely chopped garlic
1 teaspoon (5 g) chopped thyme
2 tablespoons (30 ml) extra virgin olive oil

GARNISH

1 tablespoon (15 ml) extra virgin olive oil
¼ bunch basil, julienned

RED ONION JAM AND SHREDDED DUCK CONFIT PIZZA

Preheat oven to 500°F or 260°C.

For pizza dough, in a small bowl, dissolve yeast and water. Add honey and stir together. Let sit for 2 minutes or until water is cloudy. Add olive oil and mix well.

Place flour and salt in a food processor fitted with the blade attachment. Pulse a couple times then, with machine running, pour in yeast mixture and process until dough forms a ball. Transfer on lightly floured surface. Knead for 2 minutes adding flour as necessary until dough is smooth and elastic.

Place dough into a lightly oiled bowl. Cover with plastic wrap and let rise for 30 minutes in a warm spot.

Divide dough in 2 to 4 equal pieces. Hand roll into balls and place on a tray. Cover and let rest for 30 minutes.

Place ball on a lightly floured surface. While turning dough, press down on its center then use a rolling pin to get an even

circle (8-inches or 20 cm). Form a slightly thicker raised rim around the edge.

Brush pizza with olive oil, avoiding rims. Transfer onto an oiled pizza pan.

For onion jam, heat oil and butter in a large heavy bottom saucepan over low heat and cook onions for 30 minutes, stirring often. Add sugar and vinegar and cook for another 15 minutes or until onion is dark in color and jam-like in consistency. Season with salt and pepper. Allow to cool. Jam can be kept for 1 week once covered and refrigerated.

Remove duck legs from fat, dry with a paper towel and shred.

Sprinkle cheese evenly over crust, top with purple jam, shredded duck and fresh herbs. Drizzle with olive oil.

Bake for 10 minutes or until crust is nicely brown.

To serve, cut pizza into even slices, drizzle with olive oil and finish with basil.

Serves 4.

Johann Petutschnig,
Executive Chef, CEC, CCA

Chef Johann began his culinary career in his hometown of Klagenfurt, Austria. Prior to joining Royal Caribbean International, Johann had the honor of working for the King of Norway. Along the way, he has earned several awards from various international culinary competitions. When Johann joined Royal Caribbean International in July 2005 onboard the Navigator of the Seas, he brought with him 7 years of shipboard culinary management experience acquired while working with other cruise lines. Among his many professional credentials, he is also an American Culinary Federation certified Executive Chef and Culinary Administrator. While on vacation, Johann enjoys spending his time fishing in Norway and visiting with his family.

SCALLOPS MARINADE

¼ cup (60 ml) extra virgin olive oil
½ teaspoon (2 g) chili flakes
2 cloves garlic, shaved
½ teaspoon (2 g) coriander seeds, roasted
and crushed

SCALLOPS

12 large sea scallops
6 skewers

FOCACCIA CROUTONS

½ loaf rosemary focaccia, cut into
large dice (purchased)
4 tablespoons (60 ml) extra virgin olive oil
Salt and freshly ground black pepper

VINAIGRETTE

2 tablespoons (30 g) Dijon mustard
2 cloves garlic, crushed
Juice of 1 lemon
¼ cup (60 ml) red wine vinegar
½ cup (120 ml) extra virgin olive oil
Salt and freshly ground black pepper

SALAD

6 ripe tomatoes, blanched, peeled, seeded,
cut into large dice
1 medium size red bell pepper, cubed
1 medium size green bell pepper, cubed
1 seedless cucumber, cubed
1 medium size red onion, sliced
10 basil leaves
18 kalamata olives
2 tablespoons (30 g) small capers

GARNISH

Mint leaves

PANZANELLA SALAD

Preheat oven to 380°F or 195°C.

For marinade, in a small stainless steel bowl, mix all ingredients, cover and set aside.

Pat dry scallops. Prepare scallop skewers by sliding 2 scallops per skewer. Coat with marinade, cover and refrigerate for 1 hour.

To prepare croutons place diced focaccia on a baking sheet and drizzle with olive oil. Toss well to coat evenly. Season to taste with salt and black pepper. Bake for 5 minutes or until crisp. Set aside to cool on a paper towel.

To grill scallops:

Outdoor grill: Heat to medium high. Brush scallops with the remaining marinade and place on the grill. Cook each side for 2 minutes, turning only once. Remove from the grill and set aside.

Indoor grill: Lightly oil a grill pan. Set temperature to medium/high heat. Brush scallops with the remaining marinade and place on the pan. Cook each side for approximately 5 minutes, turning only once. Remove and set aside.

For vinaigrette, place mustard, garlic, lemon juice, vinegar and olive oil in a blender. Season to taste and blend until smooth and emulsified. Allow to rest.

To make salad, place all ingredients into a large glass bowl, add diced focaccia and ½ of the dressing. Mix lightly.

Place salad on chilled plates. Top with scallop skewers and garnish with mint leaves.

Serve remaining dressing on the side.

Serves 6.

CULINARY NOTE:

You can find stainless steel skewers at any department, grocery or kitchen equipment store. They are durable, reusable and easy to clean. If you use bamboo or wooden skewers, try soaking them in water for a few hours first. The moisture will keep them from burning too quickly.

DRESSING

Juice of 1 lemon
⅓ cup (90 ml) red wine vinegar
1 cup (250 ml) extra virgin olive oil
1 tablespoon (15 g) julienned basil
1 teaspoon (5 g) oregano
Salt and freshly ground black pepper

SHRIMP

1 tablespoon (15 g) unsalted butter
1 tablespoon (15 ml) extra virgin olive oil
2 cloves garlic, minced

24 large size shrimp, peeled, deveined and tails
left on (size 16/20)
¼ bunch parsley, finely chopped
Salt and freshly ground black pepper

SALAD

3 heads romaine lettuce, washed, dried and
cut crosswise
3 tomatoes, cut in wedges
2 seedless cucumbers, cut in half lengthwise
then thickly sliced

¾ pound (350 g) feta cheese, cubed
1 small red onion, cut in wedges
24 green olives, seeded
24 kalamata olives
¼ bunch basil, julienned
Salt and freshly ground black pepper

WARM GRILLED SHRIMP GREEK SALAD

For dressing, in a small non-reactive bowl, mix lemon juice and vinegar. Slowly whisk in olive oil. Add herbs and season with salt and black pepper to taste. Cover and refrigerate.

For shrimp, in a cast iron pan over high heat, warm butter and olive oil, add garlic and sauté for 1 minute. Add shrimp and sauté for 4 minutes or until they turn pink. Add parsley and season with salt and black pepper.

To make salad, toss all ingredients with vinaigrette, season to taste and serve in chilled bowls. Crown with shrimp and finish with freshly ground black pepper.

Serves 6.

Appetizers

4 cloves garlic, crushed
1/2 cup (120 ml) extra virgin olive oil
Salt and freshly ground black pepper

GRILLED VEGETABLES

*2 Portabella mushrooms, trimmed and
cut into 6 wedges*
*1 yellow zucchini, trimmed and
cut into 1/2 inch (1.2 cm) slices*
*1 green zucchini, trimmed and
cut into 1/2 inch (1.2 cm) slices*

ROASTED GARLIC

1 head colossal garlic
Extra virgin olive oil
Salt and freshly ground pepper

PESTO

1/2 cup (120 g) pine nuts
3 cups (700 g) loosely packed fresh basil leaves
3 large cloves garlic
1/4 cup (60 g) coarsely grated Parmesan cheese
1 teaspoon (5 g) salt
1 teaspoon (5 g) freshly ground black pepper
2/3 cup (150 ml) extra virgin olive oil

TOMATOES

3 tablespoons (45 ml) extra virgin olive oil
3 tablespoons (45 ml) balsamic vinegar
15 cherry tomatoes

1/2 cantaloupe, sliced into 6 wedges
1/4 pound (120 g) prosciutto, thinly sliced

GARNISH

6 bread sticks of your choice
Frisée lettuce

GRILLED VEGETABLE ANTIPASTI

In a small bowl, mix all ingredients for marinade. Place mushrooms in a small flat dish and pour marinade over. Refrigerate for at least 3 hours. Reserve a little marinade for remaining vegetables.

Preheat oven to 325°F or 165°C.

To roast garlic, cut head into six 1/2-inch-thick slices (1.2 cm). Rub with some oil and season to taste. Place in an ovenproof dish, sprinkle with a little water and cover with aluminum foil. Roast for 30 minutes or until tender.

For pesto, in a small skillet over high heat, toss pine nuts, taking care not to burn them.

In a food processor, combine garlic, basil and pine nuts. Process until finely chopped. Add cheese, salt and pepper. With motor on low speed, slowly add olive oil a little at a time, processing until well blended and stopping several times to scrape down the sides.

To grill the vegetables:

Outdoor grill: Heat to medium high. Brush cut sides of vegetables with remaining marinade and place on grill. Cook each slice for 3 to 5 minutes, turning only once. Remove from grill and set aside.

Indoor grill: Lightly oil a grill pan. Set temperature to medium/high heat. Brush cut sides of vegetables with remaining marinade and place on pan. Cook each slice for approximately 5 minutes, turning only once. Remove and set aside.

In a mixing bowl, combine oil and vinegar, add tomatoes, salt and pepper to taste. Toss well.

Wrap cantaloupe with prosciutto.

To serve, arrange grilled vegetables, cantaloupe, balsamic tomatoes and roasted garlic on chilled plates.

Drizzle with pesto and garnish with bread sticks and bouquet of frisée.

Serves 6.

Jozef Lisner, Executive Chef, CEC

Chef Jozef comes to us from the Netherlands. He first started studying aviation engineering then decided to follow his real passion, cooking. After his graduation from one of the most famous Hotel & Restaurant Schools in Europe, Chef Jozef worked in some of the leading restaurants and hotels in the Netherlands. His love of travel and new challenges drove him to work all over Europe and the Middle East. He joined Royal Caribbean International in 2004 as an Executive Sous Chef and was soon promoted to Executive Chef. In his free time, he enjoys long walks on the beach, traveling and reading.

MOUSSE BASE

1/3 cup (85 g) butter
1/3 cup (85 g) all-purpose flour
4 cups (1 l) milk
1/4 bunch basil leaves
1/2 stalk lemongrass
1 fresh Serrano Chile, cut in half
1 tablespoon (15 ml) soy sauce

2.2 pounds (1 k) medium shrimp, peeled, deveined, tail off (31/40)
1/2 pound (250 g) cod fillet, skin off
Salt and freshly ground white pepper

1/4 cup (60 ml) heavy cream
1 egg yolk
Juice of 1/2 lemon

COATING

1 egg, beaten
1/4 cup (60 g) all-purpose flour
1/3 cup (85 g) breadcrumbs
2 cups (500 ml) vegetable oil for frying

DUTCH BITTERBALLEN WITH A TWIST

To make mousse, prepare the roux by melting butter in a small sauce pan over low heat. Add flour a little at the time stirring constantly. Cook for 4 minutes. Do not brown.

For seafood, in a large saucepan or medium size stockpot, warm milk and stir in all ingredients. Bring to a boil and simmer for 15 minutes.

Strain liquid and gently add to roux. Stir for about 5 minutes or until sauce is smooth and has thickened.

Season with salt and pepper and let cool.

Meanwhile, dice shrimp and cod. Transfer into a stainless steel or glass bowl and mix with cream, egg yolk and lemon juice. Add to milk mixture. Transfer into a greased shallow pan, cover and refrigerate overnight.

Divide mixture into 16 equal parts. With wet hands, shape mixture into balls. Roll balls in flour then dip in egg and finally roll in breadcrumbs.

Pour oil in a frying pan and heat over medium heat to 320°F or 160°C. Fry fish balls for 2 minutes or until golden. Using a slotted spoon, remove from oil and drain strips on a paper-lined plate.

Serve immediately with your favorite dip.

Makes 16 mini balls.

Ingredients

GARLIC OIL
1/4 cup (60 ml) extra virgin olive oil
5 cloves garlic, shaved

TAPENADE
1/4 cup (60 ml) mayonnaise
1/4 cup (60 ml) sour cream
Juice of 1 lemon
1 tablespoon (15 ml) Worcestershire sauce

1/2 teaspoon (2.5 g) cayenne pepper
1/2 teaspoon (2.5 g) celery salt
12-ounce (340 g) pack cream cheese, softened
10-ounce (300 g) smoked salmon
4-ounce (115 g) smoked mackerel
4-ounce (115g) smoked trout
3 tablespoons (45 g) chopped chives
1 red bell pepper, diced
3 tablespoons (45 g) capers, drained
Salt and freshly ground white pepper

TOAST
1 French baguette, sliced 3-inches (1 cm) thick
Salt and freshly ground black pepper

GARNISH
Chive sprigs
2 lemons, sliced

SMOKED FISH TAPENADE

Preheat oven to 400°F or 205°C.

To prepare garlic oil, in a small saucepan over low heat, simmer oil and garlic for 10 minutes. Do not brown. Remove from heat and allow cooling.

To make tapenade, in a glass or stainless steel bowl, combine first 7 ingredients and mix well. Gently fold in fish, chives, bell pepper and capers. Do not over mix.

Season with salt and pepper. Cover and refrigerate.

Brush bread slices with garlic oil. Place on a baking sheet. Season with salt and pepper. Bake for 2 minutes or until golden and crispy. Set aside to cool on a paper towel.

To serve, divide fish tapenade into individual chilled ramekins. Garnish with chive sprigs and lemon slices.

Serves 6.

CULINARY NOTES:

Why use white pepper? Black pepper has a more pronounced, spicy flavor with a floral aroma. It can be somewhat overpowering in delicate sauces. White sauces and soups are typically seasoned with white pepper in order to derive the proper flavor without leaving large flecks of black pepper in the finished item.

GARLIC BUTTER

1/2 cup (120 g) butter, softened
1/4 cup (60 g) margarine, softened
3 cloves garlic, minced
1 anchovy fillet, minced
1/2 teaspoon (2 ml) Worcestershire sauce
1/2 teaspoon (2 ml) brandy
3/4 teaspoon (4 ml) freshly squeezed lemon juice
3 tablespoons (45 g) chopped fresh parsley
1 egg yolk
Salt and freshly ground white pepper

1 (10-ounce) (250 to 300g) can snails

GLAZE

1/2 cup (120 g) butter
2 shallots, chopped
2 cloves garlic, chopped
3 tablespoons (45 g) chopped parsley
1/2 teaspoon (2 g) chopped rosemary
1/2 teaspoon (2 g) chopped thyme
1 tablespoon (15 ml) veal demi-glace (page 159)
2 tablespoons (30 ml) red wine
1/2 teaspoon (2 ml) brandy
Salt and freshly ground white pepper

ESCARGOT BOURGUIGNONNE

For garlic butter, combine softened butter and margarine in a food processor and whip continuously, while adding all other ingredients except for the yolk. Continue processing for 3 minutes, until all ingredients are combined and mixture is light and airy. Add the egg yolk and adjust seasoning with salt and pepper. Process for 30 seconds more. Transfer butter mixture to a small bowl and set aside.

Rinse and drain snails, then pat dry.

For glaze, melt butter in a sauté pan over medium heat and sauté shallots and garlic for 3 minutes. Add herbs, veal demi-glace, red wine and brandy and simmer for 5 to 7 minutes until reduced to a glaze consistency. Add snails and sauté for 2 minutes or until they are heated through. Adjust seasoning with salt and pepper. Remove from heat and let cool.

Preheat oven to 400°F or 200°C.

Transfer snails to snail plate. Cover snails completely with butter mixture.

Bake for 5 minutes or until snails are hot and butter is completely melted and brown on top.

Serve immediately with slices of freshly baked bread.

Serves 4.

CULINARY NOTES:

There are three principal types of edible snails grown in Europe: Petit Gris (Helix Aspersa), Burgundy or Vineyard (Helix Pomatia) and Turkish Edible (Helix Lucorum). The Burgundy snail is the most popular. They grow to be about 1 3/4 inches (4.5 cm) and have a slightly herbal flavor. The Petit Gris is smaller and possesses a fuller, nuttier taste. Petit Gris snails are beginning to be cultivated in the United States partly because they are not as difficult to raise as the Burgundy variety.

8 (3 1/2 to 4-inch) (7.5 to 10 cm)
squares puff pastry, purchased
1 egg, lightly beaten
2 tablespoons (30 g) poppy seeds
2 tablespoons (30 g) sesame seeds

FILLING

1/2 cup (120 g) butter
2 shallots, chopped
2 cloves garlic, chopped
1/2 cup (120 g) crimini mushrooms, sliced
1/2 cup (120 g) white or button mushrooms, sliced
1/2 cup (120 g) shiitake mushrooms, sliced
1/2 cup (120 g) oyster mushrooms
1 cup (250 ml) white wine
1/4 cup (60 ml) heavy cream
1/4 cup (60 ml) veal demi-glace (page 159)
1 teaspoon (5 g) chopped thyme
Salt and freshly ground black pepper

GARNISH

1/2 red bell pepper, finely diced
1/3 cup chives, finely chopped

WILD MUSHROOM FEUILLETÉE

Preheat oven to 375°F or 190°C.

Grease a baking sheet with butter.

Place pastry squares on baking sheet and brush with beaten egg. Sprinkle, diagonally, half one side with poppy seeds and the other half with sesame seeds. Bake for 15 minutes or until golden and puffed.

In a large sauté pan, over medium heat, melt butter. Add shallots and cook until translucent, about 3 minutes. Add garlic and mushrooms and sauté until liquid is almost evaporated. Season with salt and pepper. Remove mushrooms from pan, leaving the liquid.

Place pan back on the heat, add wine, cream, demi-glace and thyme; simmer for 4 minutes. Return mushrooms to pan and adjust seasoning.

Split pastry squares horizontally into top and bottom halves. Place on warmed plates. Spoon mushroom mixture on each bottom half and cover with top half.

Garnish with bell peppers and chives.

Serves 4.

CULINARY NOTES:

Making puff pastry dough is a rather complex undertaking and will produce less than satisfactory results if the procedure is not followed exactly.

The good news is there are a number of high quality frozen puff pastry products on the market today that eliminate the need to make a batch at home.

Frozen pastry sheets usually come folded in half and you need to thaw them completely to unfold. If you remove the sheet from the package, slightly spread apart the two halves and place on a baking sheet so it looks like a tent, the sheet will thaw without cracking down the center. This way you will have a complete sheet instead of two broken halves.

Ivo Christoph Jahn, Executive Chef, CEC

Chef Ivo joined Royal Caribbean International in February 2004 as Executive Chef. Born in Biedenkopf, Germany he began his culinary career in 1986 working for the Waitz Hotel in Frankfurt. He then traveled through Europe working for some of the best Michelin Star restaurants including Traube Tonbach and Domschenke Billerbeck. In 1999 he completed his Master Chef Certification at the Hotel School in Altötting. He began his cruise career working for Silver Seas and Celebrity Cruises prior to joining Royal Caribbean International. When not sailing he enjoys going out with friends, fishing and playing golf.

SALMON MOUSSE

4 ounces (120 g) fresh salmon, skinned and diced
1 egg
1/2 cup (120 ml) heavy cream
Juice of 1 lemon
Salt and freshly ground white pepper

FISH

3 Dover soles, 1 pound (450 g) each,
skin off, filleted
12 large size shrimp, peeled, deveined and
tails off (size 16/20)
12 wooden toothpicks
1 tablespoon (15 g) butter
1 shallot, finely diced
1/3 cup (90 ml) white wine
1 cup (250 ml) fish stock (page 158)

SAUCE

2 tablespoons (30 ml) extra virgin olive oil
2 shallots, finely diced
2 cloves garlic, finely chopped
1/2 pound (250 g) potatoes, cubed
1/4 cup (60 g) fresh arugula, cleaned, stems off
1/4 cup (60 g) fresh spinach, cleaned, stems off
1/4 cup (60 ml) white wine
1 cup (250 ml) vegetable stock (page 158)
2 tablespoons (30 ml) sour cream
Salt and freshly ground white pepper

GARNISH

1 tablespoon (15 ml) extra virgin olive oil
1 cup (250 g) grape tomatoes
Salt and freshly ground black pepper

DOVER SOLE ROLLS
Arugula-potato sauce and tomato compote

Preheat oven to 300°F or 150°C.

For mousse, place salmon and egg in a blender, run for 3 minutes at medium speed. Slowly add cream, lemon juice, salt and pepper. Beat at medium speed until all ingredients are mixed together, scraping sides occasionally.

Arrange sole fillets on a baking pan, pat dry and spread a thin layer of salmon mousse over each fillet; top with shrimp and roll.

"Close" sole fillets with a toothpick to keep in shape. Set aside.

In a sauté pan over medium heat, melt butter and sauté shallots for 3 minutes until translucent; add wine and fish stock and bring to a boil. Place sole rolls into a 12 inch by 8 inch (30 x 20 cm) baking pan, cover with liquid mixture and bake for 15 minutes.

For sauce, in a sauté pan over medium heat, warm olive oil and sauté shallots and garlic for 3 minutes, add potatoes and sauté for 10 minutes or until potatoes are golden. Add arugula, spinach, white wine and vegetable stock, season to taste and bring to a boil. Reduce heat and simmer for 10 minutes or until potatoes are soft. Place mixture into a blender and blend until smooth. Pass sauce through a sieve and keep warm. Just before serving whisk in sour cream.

In a sauté pan over high heat, warm oil and sauté tomatoes for 2 minutes or until tomatoes burst open. Season with salt and pepper.

Cut sole rolls diagonally. Place rolls in the center of warmed deep plates. Surround with sauce and garnish with tomato compote.

Serves 6.

PIQUILLO PEPPERS

2 piquillo peppers
3 tablespoons (30 ml) extra virgin olive oil
1 clove garlic, shaved

PIPERADE

2 tablespoons (30 ml) extra virgin olive oil
4-ounce (120 g) Parma ham,
cut into ½-inch (1.3 cm) squares
1 yellow onion, chopped
1 clove garlic, minced
1 red bell pepper, sliced lengthwise into strips
1 green bell pepper, sliced lengthwise into strips
3 tablespoons (45 ml) dry white wine
1 tablespoon (15 g) chopped basil
1 tablespoon (15 g) chopped parsley
⅓ cup (90 ml) chicken stock (page 158)
5-ounce (140 g) cherry tomatoes, halved
1 teaspoon (5 g) sweet paprika
Salt and freshly ground black pepper

HALIBUT

6 (3-ounce) (86 g) skinned halibut fillets
1 bunch basil
2 tablespoons (30 ml) extra virgin olive oil
Juice of 1 lemon
Salt and freshly ground white pepper

SHRIMP

6 large shrimp, raw, peeled and deveined
(size 16/20 or U 12)
1 tablespoon (15 g) butter
Juice of 1 lemon
Salt and freshly ground pepper

HALIBUT AND SHRIMP WITH PIPERADE

Preheat oven to 350°F or 175°C.

Place oil-rubbed piquillo peppers in an ovenproof baking dish and roast in the oven for 10 minutes. Let cool, peel, deseed, cut in thin strips and transfer into a glass bowl. Gently mix with garlic and remaining olive oil and refrigerate for 2 hours.

For piperade, in a sauté pan over medium heat, warm oil and sauté ham for 8 minutes or until golden. Remove to a plate with a slotted spoon.

Using the same pan, sauté onion and garlic for 3 minutes. Add peppers and sauté for 2 minutes. Deglaze with wine, stir in fresh herbs and chicken stock. Season with salt and pepper and simmer for 10 minutes or until peppers are soft, stirring occasionally.

Add cherry tomatoes, browned ham and paprika and cook, uncovered for 7 to 10 minutes or until juices have thickened and vegetables are melting.

Pat dry halibut, season with salt and pepper and loosely wrap into basil leaves.

In a sauté pan over medium heat, warm half of the olive oil and sauté halibut for 3 minutes, turning once. Transfer into an ovenproof baking dish and drizzle with remaining oil and lemon juice. Place in the oven with the door ajar to keep warm.

Sauté shrimp in butter in a sauté pan over medium/high heat for 5 minutes on all sides. Season with salt and pepper and drizzle with lemon juice. Keep warm.

Arrange halibut and shrimp on warmed appetizer plates, top with marinated piquillo peppers and finish with a couple spoonfuls of piperade.

Mark Wilson, Executive Chef, CEC

Born and raised in Waimate, New Zealand, Chef Mark completed his culinary apprenticeship at the Otago Cromwell University. His love for food drove him to work in some of the most reputed hotels and restaurants in Europe and the United States such as the Mark Hotel, the Waldorf Astoria and the Plaza Athénée where he trained under Chef Alain Ducasse. Loving to travel as much as he loves food, he then decided to try his sea legs working for Radisson Silverseas and NCL before joining the Royal Caribbean family. Being from New Zealand, Chef Mark's main hobby is Rugby, which he plays and watches regularly. He also very much enjoys cricket and squash as well as spending his free time with family and friends.

ROASTED PEPPERS
2 bell peppers
2 tablespoons (30 ml) extra virgin olive oil
Salt

MARINADE
2 cloves garlic, minced
Juice of 1/2 lemon
1/3 cup (90 ml) extra virgin olive oil
Salt and freshly ground black pepper
2 tablespoons (30 ml) balsamic vinegar

VEGETABLES
6 portabella caps, stalks and gills removed
12 asparagus, peeled

TAPENADE DRESSING
1/2 cup (120 ml) balsamic vinegar
1 tablespoon (15 g) brown sugar
1 (5-ounce) (150 g) jar chunky black olive tapenade, purchased

TOAST
1/4 cup (60 g) butter, softened and whipped
2 cloves garlic, minced
1 teaspoon (5 ml) fresh lemon juice
1 tablespoon (15 g) grated Parmesan cheese
1 teaspoon (5 g) chopped parsley

1 baguette, sliced
3 1/2 ounces (100 g) goat cheese, softened
Freshly ground black pepper
Fresh thyme

GARNISH
Frisée lettuce

CHAR-GRILLED PORTABELLA CAPS

Preheat oven to 400°F or 200°C.

Place peppers in an ovenproof dish, drizzle with oil, season with salt and roast for 20 minutes or until brown and blistery. Remove peppers from oven, place them into a small bowl and cover with plastic wrap. A small, tightly closed paper bag will also do. This loosens the skins and eases peeling. Peel and cut lengthwise.

For marinade, combine all ingredients in a small stainless steel bowl and mix well. Brush portabella caps with ¾ of the marinade.

To grill portabella mushrooms, heat a grilling pan over high heat. Sear each side of the mushrooms for approximately 3 minutes or until cooked. Transfer onto a baking sheet, top with roasted pepper strips and remaining marinade. Cover and keep warm.

Blanch asparagus in boiling, salted water for 3 minutes. Cool in ice water, drain and set aside. Reheat in hot water for a few seconds, just prior to serving.

For tapenade dressing, in a small saucepan over medium to low heat, reduce balsamic vinegar and sugar by half. Transfer ¾ of the glaze into a small stainless steel bowl and let cool. Add olive tapenade and mix well. Cover and refrigerate.

Keep remaining glaze in a small glass bowl to be used for finishing touches.

In a small stainless steel bowl, mix butter, garlic, lemon juice, Parmesan cheese and parsley. Spread butter mixture over slices of baguettes and pan-fry until golden brown turning over once. Spread baguette slices with goat cheese. Sprinkle with pepper and thyme and keep warm.

To serve, place portabella mushrooms in the center of warm appetizer plates, top with asparagus, goat cheese crouton and a bouquet of frisée. Drizzle with tapenade dressing.

Finish with a few drops of balsamic glaze around each plate.

Serves 6.

ASIAN SOY DRESSING

¼ cup (60 ml) fish sauce
½ cup (120 ml) sweet soy sauce
¾ cup (175 ml) lime juice
¼ cup (60 ml) vegetable oil
1 cup (250 ml) water
1 tablespoon (15 g) finely chopped ginger
2 cloves garlic, minced
3 tablespoons (45 g) sugar
4 tablespoons (60 g) honey
1 fresh chili, finely chopped
2 tablespoons (30 ml) sesame oil

1 tablespoon (15 g) cornstarch

1 tablespoon (15 g) chopped cilantro

TARTAR

2 pounds (1 kg) yellowfin tuna (Toro A1 sushi grade), small dice
Juice of 2 limes

VEGETABLES

18 pieces small shiitake mushrooms
24 snow peas
1 avocado, peeled, sliced and placed in cold, lemony water

GARNISH

6 ounces (170 g) Alfalfa sprouts
10 red radishes, julienned
½ plum tomato, peeled, seeded and julienned

AVOCADO AND YELLOWFIN TUNA TARTAR

For Asian dressing, combine all ingredients with the exception of cilantro and cornstarch. Whisk well. Place ¾ of the dressing in a stainless steel bowl, cover and refrigerate.

To make sauce, in a small saucepan over medium heat, bring remaining Asian dressing to a boil, add cornstarch a little at a time until sauce coats the spoon. Strain, cover and refrigerate. Upon serving, add cilantro to the sauce.

In a stainless steel bowl, marinate tuna in the cold Asian dressing and lime juice. Cover and refrigerate for 20 minutes.

Sauté mushrooms in a hot saucepan with 2 tablespoons of dressing for 1 minute.

Blanch snow peas in boiling salted water for 2 minutes. Cool in ice water, drain and julienne. Keep refrigerated.

To serve, place tuna tartar in the center of chilled plates. Top with shiitake mushrooms, julienned snow peas and avocado. Finish with Alfalfa sprouts and julienned radishes and tomato.

Drizzle with Asian sauce.

Served on the side, the spiciness of pickled ginger will enhance the taste of the marinated tuna.

Serves 6.

CULINARY NOTES:

Each part of the tuna fish differs in quality and therefore in price. There are five main cuts to be found on the open market: Otoro, Jutoro, Akami, Belly Cut and Back Cut. Similar to beef sold in the United States, tuna is graded based on the fat content (marbling) found within the meat. Otoro or Toro grade has the highest level of fat and is the most expensive.

PUMPKIN

¹/4 cup (60 ml) extra virgin olive oil
¹/2 teaspoon (5 g) ground cumin
¹/2 teaspoon (5 g) cayenne pepper
¹/2 teaspoon (5 g) salt
¹/2 teaspoon (5 g) freshly ground black pepper
2 pounds (1 kg) pumpkin or butternut squash, skin
removed and cut into ³/4 inch (2 cm) cubes

DRESSING

1 tablespoon (15 ml) red wine vinegar
1 shallot, finely sliced
¹/4 cup (60 ml) extra virgin olive oil
Salt and freshly ground black pepper

FETA CHEESE

5¹/2-ounce (150 g) store bought feta cheese,
drained and cubed

¹/2 teaspoon (5 g) red chili flakes
¹/2 teaspoon (5 g) fresh thyme leaves
1 tablespoon (15 ml) extra virgin olive oil
Salt and freshly ground black pepper

SPINACH

12-ounce (340 g) baby spinach, stems removed
20 kalamata olives, pitted

ROASTED PUMPKIN SALAD

Preheat oven to 350°F or 175°C.

In a large stainless steel bowl, place olive oil, cumin, cayenne pepper, salt and pepper and stir to combine. Add cubed pumpkin and mix well to coat all pieces with oil mixture.

Transfer pumpkin to a sheet pan or roasting pan and bake for 30 minutes or until lightly caramelized and tender.

For dressing, in a small non-reactive bowl, mix vinegar and shallot. Slowly whisk in olive oil. Season with salt and pepper to taste. Cover and refrigerate.

Marinate feta cheese with all ingredients in a small stainless steel bowl. Cover and refrigerate.

Arrange spinach, pumpkin and feta cheese into chilled plates. Garnish with kalamata olives and drizzle with dressing.

Serves 4.

DIP

1 teaspoon (5 ml) extra virgin olive oil
1 medium yellow onion, diced
3 cloves garlic, chopped

12-ounce (340 g) baby spinach, shredded

1 cup (250 g) ricotta cheese
1 (8-ounce) (230 g) package
cream cheese, softened
14-ounce (400 g) thawed, frozen
artichoke hearts, chopped
Salt and freshly ground white pepper

GARNISH

1 cup (230 g) shredded Cheddar cheese

TORTILLA CHIPS

1 cup (240 ml) canola oil, for frying
1 (14-ounce) (400g) package
store bought small diameter corn tortillas,
cut into 6 equal wedges
Salt

ARTICHOKE AND SPINACH DIP

Preheat oven to 350°F or 175°C.

For the dip, in a saucepan over medium heat, warm oil and sauté onion and garlic for 4 minutes. Do not brown. Add baby spinach and sauté for 2 minutes.

Remove from heat and stir in ricotta and cream cheese. Mix well.

Add artichokes and season with salt and pepper.

Divide mixture equally into oven-proof serving ramekins.

Top with cheddar cheese and bake for 15 minutes.

For tortilla chips, in a frying pan over medium/high heat, warm oil and fry a few chips at a time, for 1 minute or until golden, turning once, using a slotted spoon. Drain chips on a paper-lined plate. Season with salt.

The perfect dip to share with friends.

Serves 8.

PIE

1 pie crust purchased or
1 cup (250 g) all-purpose flour
1/2 teaspoon (5 g) salt
1/4 cup shortening (60 g), room temperature
3 tablespoons (45 ml) water

3 tablespoons (45 ml) extra virgin olive oil
1 cup julienned Vidalia onion (3 large onions)
1 tablespoon (15 g) chopped thyme
Salt and freshly ground black pepper
1/2 cup (120 g) shredded Gruyère cheese

FILLING

3 eggs
1/3 cup (90 ml) heavy cream
1 tablespoon (15 g) chopped parsley
1 tablespoon (15 g) chopped chives
1/2 teaspoon (2 g) ground nutmeg
Salt and freshly ground black pepper

RED PEPPER COULIS

4 red bell peppers
1 tablespoon (15 ml) extra virgin olive oil
Salt and freshly ground black pepper

GARNISH

1 medium Vidalia onion
1/3 cup (90 ml) vegetable oil
Fresh chervil

VIDALIA ONION TART

Preheat oven to 350°F or 180°C.

In a medium bowl, with a fork, lightly stir together flour and salt. With fork, cut shortening into flour until the mixture resembles coarse crumbs. Sprinkle cold water one teaspoon at a time, mixing lightly with fork after each addition, until pastry begins to hold together. With your hands, shape pastry into a ball. Refrigerate for 30 minutes.

On a lightly floured surface, roll pastry in 1/8-inch (0.32 cm) thick circle about 2-inches (5 cm) larger all around than pie mold.

Roll pastry circle gently onto rolling pin. Transfer to pie mold and unroll. With a sharp knife, trim edges, pinch to form a high edge and make a decorative edge by pressing it with a fork. Prick crust with a fork to prevent puffing during baking. Refrigerate for 1/2 hour.

Blind bake pie crust for 7 minutes, remove from oven and let cool.

While crust is baking, warm olive oil in a small saucepan over medium heat and sauté onions until translucent, about 4 minutes. Add thyme and season with salt and pepper.

Spread onions evenly in pie crust. Sprinkle with cheese.

In a medium bowl beat eggs lightly, add cream, fresh herbs and seasonings. Beat until well mixed.

Pour mixture over cheese and onions. Bake for 40 minutes.

For coulis, blanch peppers in boiling water for 5 minutes. Cool in ice water and remove skins.

In a blender, purée the peppers and olive oil until smooth. Season with salt and pepper.

For garnish, in a small skillet over high heat, warm oil and deep fry onion until golden brown, about 2 minutes.

Serve slices of tart on warmed plates, top with fried onions and garnish with spoons of pepper coulis.

Serves 6.

CULINARY NOTES:

Vidalia onions thrive in the sandy soil and mild conditions found in southeastern Georgia. Nowhere else on earth can a Vidalia onion be grown that will produce the same sweetness for which this onion is so famous. Several attempts have been made to cultivate it in other parts of the country, but the results have always been the same; hot, not sweet.

Soups

SUGAR SYRUP

1/4 cup (60 g) sugar
1/4 cup (60 ml) water

CHILLED SOUP

1 cup (250 ml) freshly squeezed orange juice
1/4 cup (60 g) fresh or frozen blueberries
1/4 cup (60 g) fresh or frozen strawberries
1/4 cup (60 g) fresh or frozen raspberries
1 shot crème de cassis liqueur
1/4 cup (60 ml) club soda
1/2 cup (120 ml) buttermilk

CHILLED FOREST BERRY AND BUTTERMILK SOUP

In a small saucepan, mix sugar and water over medium heat and simmer until sugar is dissolved. Cover and refrigerate.

In a food processor, blend juice and berries. Adjust sweetness by adding sugar syrup as needed. Add crème de cassis.

Just before serving, add club soda to give the soup a sparkling twist.

Serve in chilled soup bowls and finish with a swirl of buttermilk.

Serves 6.

CULINARY NOTES:

The most complicated step in this recipe is making the sugar syrup. Don't let the sugar and water mixture boil, as the sugar will start to caramelize. Once cooled the sugar syrup can be stored in a plastic bottle for several days for use in a variety of other recipes and bar mixes.

CHILLED SOUP

1 small stick cinnamon
1 clove
1 sprig fresh thyme

5 apples, peeled cored and cubed
3 large carrots, peeled and cubed
1 teaspoon (5 g) ground nutmeg

$^1/_2$ teaspoon (2.5 g) lemon zest
Juice of half lemon
2 cups (480 ml) apple juice

$^1/_2$ cup (115 g) apple sauce

$^1/_4$ cup (60 ml) Champagne or sparkling wine

GARNISH

2 tablespoons (30 g) coarse white sugar
1 teaspoon (5 g) ground cinnamon
$^1/_3$ cup (85 g) sour cream
1 small carrot, peeled and julienned
Chervil sprigs

CHILLED APPLE AND CARROT SOUP

Wrap cinnamon, clove and thyme in a cheesecloth sachet.

In a saucepan over medium heat, combine all ingredients except apple sauce and Champagne and simmer for 20 minutes or until both carrots and apples are soft to the touch.

Discard spice sachet and transfer mixture into a food processor. Blend until smooth. Add apple sauce and mix well.

Refrigerate in a glass or stainless steel bowl for 4 hours.

Finish the soup by incorporating Champagne.

In a small glass or stainless steel bowl, mix sugar and cinnamon together.

Ladle soup into chilled bowls. Garnish with a dollop of sour cream sprinkled with cinnamon sugar and finish with julienned carrot and chervil.

Serves 6.

CULINARY NOTES:

A sachet is a cheesecloth bundle filled with aromatic ingredients used to flavor stocks, sauces and other liquids. The advantage of using a sachet is that it will allow the ingredients to infuse the hot liquid without small bits of unwanted material being left behind for you to fish out later. Examples of sachet ingredients are peppercorns and bay leafs, fresh herbs and garlic, etc.

To make a sachet simply cut a small square of cheese cloth, place the ingredients in the center and bundle the edges together like a coin purse. Tie with a long piece of Butcher's twine. Tie one end of the twine to the handle of the pot so the sachet can be easily retrieved when needed.

CHOWDER

1 tablespoon (15 g) butter
6-ounces (140 g) skinless, salt pork, diced small
2 yellow onions, diced
2 stalks celery, diced
2 tablespoons (30 g) flour
1 (51-ounce) (445g) can chopped sea clams,
drained and water reserved

3 large potatoes, peeled and diced
2 bay leaves
2 teaspoons (10 g) salt
1/4 teaspoon (1 g) celery salt
1/4 teaspoon (1 g) freshly ground white pepper

3 cups (700 ml) milk or Half & Half

GARNISH

Parsley sprigs
2 tablespoons (30 g) chopped parsley
1 teaspoon (5 g) paprika

New England Clam Chowder

To make the chowder, in a large saucepan or small stockpot melt butter and sauté bacon for 5 minutes over low heat. Add onion and celery and cook for 5 minutes or until tender. Stir flour into bacon/onion mixture and whisk until well blended and all lumps are removed.

Add enough water to clam juice to make 2 cups (500 ml) and gradually incorporate to bacon mixture, stirring constantly until thickened.

Add potatoes, bay leaves and spices. Cover and simmer for 10 minutes or until potatoes are tender.

Add clams and milk and heat thoroughly, about 5 minutes.

Remove bay leaves and ladle soup into individual soup bowls.

Garnish with freshly chopped parsley and sprinkle with paprika.

Serve chowder with your favorite crackers.

Serves 8.

CHILLED SOUP

2 medium tomatoes
2 red bell peppers
4 tablespoons (60 ml) extra virgin olive oil
2 shallots, finely chopped
8 ounces (230 g) canned pimentos
1 slice white bread, crumbled
1/2 tablespoon (10 ml) balsamic vinegar
3 cups (700 ml) tomato juice
Salt and freshly ground black pepper

SCALLOPS

6 jumbo scallops
1 tablespoon (15 ml) virgin olive oil
Salt and freshly ground black pepper

AVOCADO TOWER

2 avocados, peeled and chopped
Juice of 1 lemon

GARNISH

1/4 bunch basil, finely julienned

ZUPPA FREDDA AI POMODORI E PEPERONI DOLCI CON CAPESANTE ED AVOCADO
Chilled Red Bell Pepper Soup and Avocado Tartar

Preheat oven to 350°F or 180°C.

Fill a small pan with water and bring to a boil. Using a sharp knife, gently tear the skin of the tomatoes lengthwise in a couple of spots and place in the boiling water for about 3 minutes. Place tomatoes in ice water for 2 minutes or until the skin starts separating from the tomato. Peel, cut in half and take off seeds using a small spoon. Slice and dice tomatoes.

Place the red peppers in an ovenproof dish, drizzle with 2 tablespoons (30 ml) of olive oil. Roast for 20 minutes or until brown and blistery. Remove peppers from oven. Place them into a small bowl and cover with plastic wrap. A small, tightly closed paper bag will do also. This loosens the skins and eases peeling. Peel and finely dice the peppers.

In a large pan over medium heat, warm remaining olive oil; add shallots and sauté for about 3 minutes or until shallots are tender and translucent. Add pimentos and sauté for 3 minutes. Add bread crumbs, vinegar, tomatoes and tomato juice. Transfer into a blender, including roasted peppers and blend until smooth. Adjust seasoning with salt and pepper. Cover and refrigerate for 2 hours.

Pat dry and season sea scallops. In a saucepan, over medium heat, warm oil and sauté scallops until firm and opaque, about two minutes on each side.

Peel and dice avocados. Mix with lemon juice.

Using a biscuit cutter or small round cookie cutter as a mold, tightly pack avocado in, being careful not to mash it.

Remove mold and pour an equal amount of soup in each bowl (a soup or pasta bowl may be used). Top each avocado "tower" with a sautéed jumbo scallop. Garnish each tower with julienned basil.

Serves 6.

CULINARY NOTES:

Fresh scallops perish quickly when out of water, so you will most likely find them already shucked. If you come across scallops that are still in the shell, buy those as they are sure to be the freshest. When shopping for scallops, look for a pearly off-white or pale-golden color. Bright-white scallops have been treated with chemicals to preserve freshness. Avoid! Scallops should also have a fresh, sweet smell. Spoiled scallops smell like sulfur.

SOUP

2 cups (500 g) white cannellini beans
1/2 cup (120 g) pearled barley

2 tablespoons (30 ml) extra virgin olive oil
1/4 cup (60 g) chopped celery
1/4 cup (60 g) chopped carrots
1 yellow onion, diced
2 cloves garlic, chopped

1 ounce (30 g) prosciutto, small dice
1 ounce (30 g) pancetta, small dice
1 slice bacon, diced
1/4 cup (60 ml) dry white wine
1-16 ounce (450 g) can of chopped tomatoes
8 cups (2 L) chicken stock (page 158)
2 each rosemary sprigs
Salt and freshly ground black pepper

GARNISH

1 plum tomato, seeded and sliced
12 Parmesan shavings
1/4 bunch Italian parsley, finely chopped
1 tablespoon (15 ml) extra virgin olive oil

ZUPPA GRAN FARO

Soak cannellini beans and pearled barley in separate glass bowls filled with cold water, overnight.

In a large saucepan or medium size stockpot, over medium heat, warm oil and sauté vegetables and garlic for 10 minutes or until lightly caramelized.

Add prosciutto, pancetta and bacon and sauté until crisp. Deglaze with white wine.

Drain cannellini beans and add to vegetable mixture. Stir in canned tomatoes and chicken stock. Add rosemary and season with salt and pepper. Bring to a boil, reduce heat and simmer for 40 minutes or until beans are tender.

In a small pan filled with salted hot water, cook barley until al dente or about 15 minutes. Strain and set aside.

Remove half of the beans from soup.

Transfer soup into a blender and blend until smooth, adding some of the reserved beans a little at a time until a thickened, chunky consistency is achieved. Adjust seasoning with salt and pepper.

Place 1 tablespoon (15g) of barley and 1 tablespoon (15 g) of beans into warmed soup bowls. Garnish with sliced tomato, Parmesan shavings and parsley.

Ladle soup into individual serving bowls. Drizzle with olive oil and sprinkle with freshly ground black pepper.

Serves 6.

CULINARY NOTES:

Pancetta is the Italian word for bacon. It is pork that has been salt-cured and spiced, and dried for 3 months (but is usually not smoked). Pancetta can be found in most delicatessens and large supermarkets.

American bacon may be substituted. However, try to find bacon that is not smoked as it will add a different flavor profile to the finished dish.

SOPA DE TORTILLA

SOUP

1 tablespoon (15 ml) extra virgin olive oil

3 cloves garlic, chopped

2 medium yellow onions, chopped

3 green onions, diced

2 fresh Ancho chili peppers or jalapeños, seeded and finely chopped

2 red bell peppers, diced

2 green bell peppers, diced

1 (16-ounce) (450 g) can chopped tomatoes with juice

1 tablespoon (15 g) tomato paste

1 tablespoon (15 g) chili powder

2 teaspoons (10 g) ground cumin

1 teaspoon (5 g) dried oregano

1/4 cup (60 g) chopped fresh cilantro

1 quart (1 L) chicken stock (page 158)

Salt and freshly ground black pepper

TORTILLAS

3 large corn tortillas, store bought

1/4 cup (60 ml) canola oil, for frying

GARNISH

1 tablespoon (15 g) finely chopped cilantro

1 cup (250 g) shredded Mexican mix cheese (Sharp Cheddar, Monterey Jack and Mozzarella) optional

---

In a large saucepan or medium size stockpot, over moderate heat, warm oil and sauté garlic, onions and chili for 4 minutes or until onion is translucent.

Add bell peppers, tomatoes and tomato paste. Sweat for 5 minutes.

Add spices and chicken stock. Season with salt and pepper and bring to a boil.

Simmer for 15 minutes or until all vegetables are tender.

Add corn just before serving.

While soup is simmering, slice tortillas into thin 1/8 of an inch or 1/2 cm strips. Heat oil in a medium size frying pan over medium/high heat and fry tortilla strips for 1 minute or until golden. Using a slotted spoon, remove from oil and drain strips on a paper-lined plate.

Ladle soup in warmed soup bowls, top with tortillas and chopped cilantro and serve with a side dish of shredded cheese.

Serves 6.

CULINARY NOTES:

Capsaicin $(CH_3)_2CHCH=CH(CH_2)_4CONHCH_2C_6H_3-4-(OH)-3-(OCH_3))$ is the active compound in chili peppers which produces the tingling, burning sensation or "heat" you feel in your mouth when you take a bite of spicy, pepper-flavored foods.

Capsaicin is a fat-soluble compound, not water-soluble. If your mouth is on fire from biting into a hot pepper don't drink water! All that will do is move the heat around your mouth. Milk is the best remedy (or ice cream). The fat in the milk will surround the capsaicin and help dissipate the sensation.

SPICE PASTE

4 dried red chilies, seeded and chopped

1 medium red onion, chopped

1 teaspoon (5 g) peeled and chopped ginger

4 stems lemongrass, white part only, sliced

2 fresh red chilies, seeded and chopped

10 macadamia nuts

2 teaspoons (10 g) shrimp paste

2 tablespoons (30 g) turmeric

2 tablespoons (30 ml) vegetable oil

PRAWN SOUP

1 pound (500 g) prawn, head on, shell on

1 1/2 quarts (1.5 L) water

1 tablespoon (15 ml) vegetable oil

2 cups (500 ml) coconut milk

8 fish balls, purchased from an Asian market

1 pound (500 g) rice noodles

GARNISH

1 cucumber, peeled, seeded and julienned

1/2 cup (120 g) bean sprouts

Nethaji Dasarathan, Executive Chef, CEC

Chef Nethaji joined Royal Caribbean International in 1989 and has served on many of the company's ships since. Nethaji was born in Madras and studied for 3 years in India where he achieved a Diploma in Catering Technology. He worked as a senior Chef de Partie for the Sheraton Hotel in India for 4 years. During his spare time, he likes photography, traveling and trying different types of cuisine.

PRAWN LAKSA

To make the paste, soak chilies in hot water for 20 minutes. Place all paste ingredients in a blender and blend for 3 minutes, until very smooth, scraping the bowl regularly.

For prawn stock, set aside 4 prawns, then peel and devein remainder, reserving heads and shells. Sauté heads and shells in a deep pan over medium heat for 5 minutes until shells and heads become deep orange and aromatic. Stir in 1 cup (250 ml) of the water and boil until water has almost evaporated. Add another cup (250 ml) of water, bring to a boil and reduce by half before adding remaining water. Bring stock to a boil and simmer for 30 minutes. In a small saucepan, cook reserved prawns with a little stock, simmering for 3 to 4 minutes, or until shrimp are pink.

Heat oil in a wok or sauté pan and cook spice paste over low heat for about 8 minutes, stirring occasionally until very aromatic. Stir in prawn stock and coconut milk. Bring to a boil, then lower the heat and simmer for 10 minutes. Add peeled prawns and sliced fish balls and simmer for another 5 minutes.

Warm reserved prawns with a little stock.

In a separate pan with boiling water, cook the noodles for 5 minutes. Drain well and serve in deep soup bowls.

Ladle the soup, prawns and fish balls over the noodles. Garnish with the cucumber and bean sprouts and top each bowl with one of the reserved prawns.

Serves 4.

GOULASH

5 slices bacon, chopped

3 pounds (1.3 kg) beef chuck, trimmed and cut into 1/2-inch (1.2 cm) cubes

2 tablespoons (30 ml) vegetable oil

4 medium yellow onions, diced

3 cloves garlic, minced

3 tablespoons (45 g) sweet Hungarian paprika

1 1/2 teaspoons (7.5 g) caraway seeds

1/3 cup (85 g) all-purpose flour

1/4 cup (60 ml) red wine vinegar

1/4 cup (60 g) tomato paste

5 cups (1.2 L) beef stock (page 159)

5 cups (1/2 L) water

1/2 teaspoon (5 g) sea salt

2 red bell peppers, diced

4 large Russet potatoes, peeled and cut into 1/2-inch (1.2 cm) cubes

GARNISH

Chopped parsley

GOULASH SOUP

In a large stockpot over medium heat, cook bacon until crisp, drain with a slotted spoon and transfer to a large bowl. Reserve bacon fat.

Using the same stockpot and remaining bacon fat, brown beef cubes in small batches over high heat. Hold batches of meat warmed until needed.

Reduce heat and warm oil. Add onions and garlic and sauté for 5 minutes or until golden, stirring occasionally. Stir in paprika, caraway seeds and flour and cook for 2 minutes. Whisk in vinegar and tomato paste and cook, whisking, for 1 minute. Add beef stock, water, salt, bell peppers, bacon and beef chuck and bring to a boil, stirring continually. Reduce heat and simmer, covered, for 45 minutes.

Within 15 minutes of the simmering process, add potatoes to soup for the remaining cooking duration. Correct seasoning with salt and pepper.

Ladle soup into warmed bowls and sprinkle with chopped parsley.

Serves 6.

Gerhard Baur, Executive Chef, CEC

Chef Gerhard was born and trained in the shadows of the picturesque Austrian Alps. After working for 9 years in 5-star hotels in Europe cooking for royalty and famous people including Her Majesty the Queen of England, Prince Charles and Lady Diana, the Sultan of Brunei, Sir Elton John and Dame Margaret Thatcher he decided to get his sea legs with Royal Caribbean International as an Executive Chef. His hobbies include the co-hosting of TV cooking shows and the writing of articles for various food magazines such as Vogue Entertaining. He also enjoys photography, sailing and playing golf.

Pasta

COCONUT LIME SAUCE

2 tablespoons (30 ml) extra virgin olive oil
2 pounds (1 kg) lobster shells and heads, chopped
2 shallots, peeled and chopped
1 clove garlic, peeled and smashed
2 celery stalks, diced
2 carrots, peeled and diced
2 large tomatoes, peeled, seeded and diced
2 tablespoons (30 g) tomato paste
2 tablespoons (30 ml) brandy
1 tablespoon (15 g) thyme sprigs
1 tablespoon (15 g) ginger, peeled and chopped
1 kaffir lime leaf or zest of 2 limes

1 tablespoon (15 g) unsalted butter
3 tablespoons (45 g) all-purpose flour
1 cup (240 ml) white wine
1/2 gallon (1.8 L) fish stock (page 158)
3 tablespoons lobster base,
store bought (if available)
2 stems lemongrass or 1 tablespoon (15 g)
lemongrass herb blend, store bought

1 (13.5 fl ounce) (400 ml) can coconut milk
1/2 pound (225 g) unsalted butter,
cut into cubes
Zest of 1 lime

GARNISH

2 leeks, cleaned, julienned,
lightly dusted with flour and deep fried
2 tablespoons (30 g) chopped Italian parsley

RAVIOLI

3 to 4 dozen large size shrimp filled ravioli,
store bought
1 tablespoon (15 g) butter

SPINACH

1 teaspoon (5 g) butter
2 cloves garlic, minced
12-ounces (340 g) fresh spinach
Salt and freshly ground white pepper

SHRIMP RAVIOLI WITH COCONUT LIME SAUCE

In a large saucepan over medium heat, warm olive oil and sauté lobster shells and heads for 3 minutes. Add shallots, garlic and vegetables and sauté for 5 minutes. Add tomato paste and deglaze with brandy.

Incorporate thyme, ginger and kaffir lime leaves. Add butter and flour and mix thoroughly. Cook for 5 minutes to ensure that flour is "cooked" and has formed a roux. Add wine and reduce by half. Add fish stock, lobster base if available and lemongrass. Bring to a boil and simmer for 1 hour.

In a frying pan over high heat, warm oil and fry leek for 1 minute or until golden. Set aside on a plate layered with absorbent paper.

While sauce is simmering, cook ravioli in a stockpot of boiling salted water for about 10 minutes or as per directions on package.

Drain well and toss with butter.

In a sauté pan over medium heat, melt butter and sauté garlic for 2 minutes. Do not brown. Add spinach and cook for 1 minute or until wilted. Season with salt and pepper.

To finish sauce strain lobster mixture through a fine sieve or cheesecloth into a glass or stainless steel bowl. Add coconut milk and slowly whisk in butter a little at a time. Add lime zest and season with salt and pepper.

If necessary, reheat ravioli by sautéing over medium heat for a few moments.

To serve, place 2 spoonfuls of spinach in the center of each warmed plate. Top with ravioli and a generous amount of lobster sauce.

Garnish with fried leeks and parsley.

Serves 6.

CULINARY NOTES:

Lobster shells and heads can be purchased at your local seafood market or fishmonger. If they do not have them on hand you may be able to have them order some for you. Lobster shells freeze well and will keep up to 6 months if wrapped air-tight.

Joachim Moeller, Executive Chef, CEC

Chef Joachim of Austria comes to us with over 16 years of professional culinary and management experience. He started his training in a family-owned restaurant in Lake Edersee, Germany, then went to work for various top Michelin Star-rated restaurants, as well as the Radisson Corporation. His first foreign destination was London, England, where he joined the Radisson Edwardian Hotel culinary team. As an Executive Chef onboard the Royal Caribbean International ships, Joachim is in charge of coaching, training and directing more than 150 cooks in order to serve more than 2,000 guests every day. When not onboard, Joachim enjoys spending time riding around Europe on his Harley Davidson® and traveling abroad.

PASTA DOUGH

3 cups (700 g) flour
8 egg yolks
1 teaspoon (5 g) salt
1 teaspoon (5 ml) extra virgin olive oil
2 to 3 tablespoons (30 to 45 ml) water
(as needed)

Semolina or all purpose flour for dusting

SAUCE

1 tablespoon (15 ml) extra virgin olive oil
3 tablespoons (45 g) butter
1 shallot, finely chopped
1/4 cup (60 ml) Grey Goose vodka
1/2 cup (120 ml) fish stock (page 158)
1/2 cup (120 ml) heavy cream
Salt and freshly ground white pepper

8 ounces (250 g) smoked salmon,
cut in thin strips

GARNISH

Dill sprigs

FRESH PASTA IN VODKA, CAVIAR AND SMOKED SALMON CREAM SAUCE

For pasta, in a food processor fitted with a steel blade, combine flour, egg yolks, salt, oil and 2 tablespoons (30 ml) water. Process at medium speed until dough holds together. Pinch dough to test it. If it's too dry, add 1 more tablespoon (15 ml) of water and process until it forms a moist ball.

Place dough onto a lightly floured surface and hand knead into a smooth ball.

Wrap in plastic and let rest at room temperature for 1 hour.

To roll out dough using a pasta roller, cut dough into four equal pieces. Set roller at widest opening. Flatten first piece of dough into a thick strip. Dust pasta roller and run pasta through the machine, one at a time. Process dough through roller 2 to 3 more times until dough is smooth and somewhat elastic. Repeat operation twice using smaller openings each time.

To roll out dough by hand, cut dough into 8 equal pieces. Roll each ball under palm for 1 minute. Place ball on a lightly floured flat surface. While turning the dough, hand press down on its center. Use a rolling pin to get a rectangular dough shape. Repeat operation as many times as necessary until dough is thin and elastic.

Cut and roll pasta as desired.

For sauce, in a heavy saucepan over medium heat, warm oil and 1 tablespoon (15 g) of butter and sauté shallot until translucent, about 3 minutes. Deglaze with vodka and reduce by half. Add fish stock and simmer for 2 minutes. Add heavy cream, season to taste with salt and pepper and simmer for 10 minutes. Do not boil. Remove from heat and whisk in remaining butter a little at a time.

While sauce is simmering, cook pasta in a stockpot of boiling salted water until al dente. Drain well and toss with olive oil.

Add smoked salmon and pasta to sauce. Toss to coat, arrange into warmed serving bowls and garnish with dill.

Serves 6.

VEGETABLES

1/4 cup (60 ml) extra virgin olive oil

3 shallots, minced

3 cloves garlic, minced

2 stalks celery, finely chopped

1/2 pound (250 g) assorted wild mushrooms such as shiitake, oyster, chanterelle and portabella, brushed clean and sliced

1 oz (30 g) dried porcini mushrooms (Cepes), chopped and soaked in 1/4 cup warm chicken stock

2 tablespoons (10 g) minced parsley

1 tablespoon (5 g) minced thyme

Salt and freshly ground white pepper

1/2 pound asparagus, trimmed, cut into 2-inch (5 cm) lengths

RISOTTO

2 cups (450 g) Arborio rice

1 cup (250 ml) Champagne or sparkling wine

8 cups (1.8 L) warm chicken stock (page 158)

2 tablespoons (30 ml) crème fraîche

4 tablespoons (60 g) Parmesan cheese, freshly grated

1 tablespoon (15 g) salted butter

GARNISH

1/2 cup (100 g) Arugula

1 (10 g) black truffle, in natural juice, shaved

ASPARAGUS AND MUSHROOM RISOTTO

In a large saucepan over medium heat, warm 1/2 of the olive oil and sauté shallots and garlic for 2 minutes. Add celery and sauté for another 2 minutes or until shallots are transparent. Do not brown.

Add wild mushrooms and cook for 5 minutes or until softened. Add chopped porcini mushrooms, parsley and thyme. Season with salt and white pepper.

Transfer mushrooms mixture to a bowl and set aside.

Using the same saucepan, warm remaining olive oil, add rice and stir well for 3 minutes until rice is translucent with a white dot in the center.

Add Champagne and stir until completely absorbed.

Add the stock one ladle at a time, stirring frequently after each addition. Wait until the stock is almost completely absorbed before adding another ladle. Reserve 1/4 cup (60 ml) stock to add at the end.

Meanwhile, blanch asparagus tips in boiling salted water for 3 minutes. Cool in ice water, drain and set aside.

After about 18 minutes, rice should be tender to the bite but still slightly firm in the center and look creamy. Add mushroom mixture and asparagus and cook until heated through.

Remove from heat and stir in crème fraîche, Parmesan cheese, butter and reserved chicken stock. Season with salt and pepper.

Serve in warm bowls and finish with fresh arugula bouquets and truffle shavings.

Eet smakelijk (Bon Appétit) as we say in the Netherlands.

Serves 6.

Marcus De Jong, Executive Chef, CEC

Born in the Netherlands, Chef Marcus started his culinary career at the tender age of 8 in his mother's kitchen. Roaming Europe for many years working in 5-star hotels and restaurants, he worked his way up through the galley ranks. Chef Marcus joined Royal Caribbean International in 2006 as an Executive Chef delighting guests daily with his and his team's culinary creations. When not onboard, he enjoys golfing, snowboarding, horseback riding and most important of all, spending time with his family.

GNOCCHI

3 pounds (1.3 kg) Idaho potatoes or Russet
potatoes, peeled
1 cup (235 g) all-purpose flour
2 egg yolks
1 tablespoon (15 g) semolina flour
Salt and freshly ground white pepper
Pinch nutmeg

2 tablespoons (30 g) melted butter

Or

4 pounds (1.8 kg) gnocchi, store bought

SAUCE

4 (6-ounce) (70 g) bone-in ham,
trimmed of fat and julienned
1/4 cup (60 ml) dry white wine
1/3 cup (90 ml) chicken stock (page 158)
3/4 cup (175 ml) heavy cream
1 cup (235 g) peas, defrosted
Salt and freshly ground white pepper

ONION CONFIT

2 medium onions, peeled and shaved
1/3 cup (90 ml) extra virgin olive oil

GARNISH

Parmigiano Reggiano cheese, shaved
1/3 bunch basil, coarsely chopped
Basil sprigs

POTATO GNOCCHI

In a small saucepan over medium heat, simmer onion in olive oil for 20 minutes. Do not brown. Allow to cool. Cover and reserve.

Place potatoes into salted, cold water, bring to a boil and cook until potatoes are easily pierced with the tip of a knife, about 15 minutes.

Spread 1/4 cup (60 g) flour on a clean, dry surface. Using a ricer, press potatoes, while still hot, over flour. Let cool. Form a well in center.

In a bowl, beat egg yolks, semolina, salt, pepper and nutmeg and pour the mixture into the well. Work potato and egg mixture together to combine, working from inside the well outward until the mixture is completely incorporated. Gently knead mixture together with both hands until it begins to form a ball. Add flour as necessary to make the dough thick enough to roll.

Roll the dough into finger-thick cylinders and cut crosswise into 1 1/2 inch pieces.

Press each piece into the curve of a flour-dusted fork and roll gently to shape the gnocchi.

For the sauce, in a sauté pan over medium heat, warm half of the onion confit and sauté ham for 2 minutes. Deglaze with wine, add chicken stock and reduce by half. Add heavy cream and simmer until sauce has thickened and coats the back of a wooden spoon. Season with salt and pepper.

In a small sauté pan over medium heat, warm remaining onion confit and sauté peas for 3 minutes. Fold into ham mixture.

Cook gnocchi in a large pot of lightly salted boiling water. When gnocchi rise to the surface, remove pot from heat, add 1 glass of cold water to stop the cooking process and remove gnocchi with a slotted spoon or skimmer. Gently toss gnocchi with melted butter into a large stainless steel bowl.

Arrange gnocchi on warmed plates. Spoon sauce over and garnish with Parmigiano Reggiano cheese shavings and basil.

Serves 6.

CULINARY NOTES:

Parmigiano Reggiano cheese is a hard-ripened, cooked (but not pressed), cow's milk cheese. Reference to this cheese dates back as far as 1348 and the manufacturing process has remained unchanged for over 7 centuries. The cheese is ripened in 75 pound (34 kg) barrel-shaped wheels for up to 24 months. A distinctive feature of this cheese is the presence of tiny crystals which result from the long ripening period. True Parmigiano Reggiano is manufactured in the Italian cheese-making plants of Parma, Reggio Emilia and Modena. You will know you have the original and best cheese if the words – Parmigiano Reggiano – are stenciled in small dots on the rind.

DOUGH

2 tablespoons (30 g) yeast
$^1/_4$ cup (60 ml) hot water
$3^1/_2$ cups (815 g) all-purpose flour
$^1/_4$ cup (60 g) salt
2 tablespoons (30 ml) extra virgin olive oil
$1^3/_4$ cups (420 ml) water, room temperature

$^1/_4$ cup (60 ml) extra virgin olive oil for drizzling

TOPPINGS

1 tablespoon (15 g) sea salt
1 tablespoon (15 g) rosemary or thyme

CLASSIC FOCACCIA

Michael Veith, Corporate Baker Chef

Chef Michael hails from Braz, Austria where he learned his trade at the Austrian School for Vocational Training for Bakery and Pastry. He is also a Master Craftsman in bakery. After working extensively in England and Austria, he decided to try his sea legs with Royal Caribbean. He now lives in London and spends a lot of time discovering England and its surroundings. When not working Chef Michael enjoys spending time with his friends mountain biking and snow boarding.

Preheat oven to 420°F or 215°C.

For dough, in a large stainless steel or glass bowl, dissolve yeast into water. Add remaining ingredients and mix well.

Divide into 4 equal pieces and place each into a separate oiled bowl. Cover each bowl with plastic wrap and let rest for 1 hour at room temperature.

Transfer dough into an oiled 12-inch (30 cm) by 18-inch (45 cm) baking pan and spread very gently with oiled fingers until desired thickness, about 1 ½-inch or 4 cm thick. Repeat with remaining dough.

Drizzle with olive oil and, using your fingers, imprint the typical holes in the dough surface. Let rest for 1 hour.

Drizzle with more oil, sprinkle with salt and fresh rosemary.

Bake for 25 minutes or until golden brown.

Makes 4 pieces.

CULINARY NOTES:

This basic bread recipe can be used as a base to make baguettes or any other type of bread.

4 (6-ounce) (170 g) halibut steaks

MARINADE
Juice of 2 lemons
2 cloves garlic, chopped
1/4 cup (60 ml) extra virgin olive oil
Salt and freshly ground black pepper

SAUCE
2 tablespoons (30 ml) vegetable oil
2 cloves garlic, chopped
2 tablespoons (30 g) Dijon mustard
2 tablespoons (30 g) all-purpose flour
1/4 cup (60 g) julienned sundried tomatoes
1 teaspoon (5 g) Cajun spice

1/4 teaspoon (1 g) paprika
1/4 teaspoon (1 ml) Tabasco® sauce
1 teaspoon (5 ml) Worcestershire sauce
Juice of 1 lime
1 cup (250 ml) chicken stock, warm (page 158)
1/2 cup (120 ml) heavy cream
Salt and freshly ground black pepper

PASTA
1 pound (450 g) dry linguini pasta
1 teaspoon (5 ml) extra virgin olive oil

GARNISH
Chopped parsley

CAJUN LINGUINI

Prepare marinade in a stainless steel bowl by combining all ingredients. Coat the fish with marinade, cover and refrigerate for 1 hour.

For sauce, in a saucepan over medium heat, warm oil and sauté garlic for 1 minute until fragrant. Add mustard and flour and stir. Add sundried tomatoes, spices, Tabasco®, Worcestershire sauce and lime juice and mix well. Slowly incorporate chicken stock a little at a time. Bring to a boil and simmer for 10 minutes. Add cream and adjust seasoning with salt and pepper. Simmer for about 7 minutes, until sauce is thick enough to coat the back of a spoon. Do not boil. Keep warm.

While sauce is simmering, cook the linguini in a stockpot of boiling salted water until al dente, about 6 to 8 minutes. Drain well and toss with the olive oil.

In a grilling pan over high heat, sear halibut steaks for 1 minute on each side, then reduce heat to medium and finish cooking for about 6 minutes or until fish is firm and opaque at the center when pierced with the tip of a small knife.

Toss pasta with sauce and place into warmed deep plates. Top with fish and finish with parsley.

Serves 4.

Stephen Yates, Senior Executive Chef, CEC

Chef Stephen joined Royal Caribbean International in January 2001. He is originally from Canada. Stephen began his culinary career at 15, working in the kitchens of the Toronto Four Seasons. Stephen has had the opportunity to work in some of the finest hotels and resorts Canada has to offer, including Chateau Whistler, Château Frontenac and Banff Springs. When not onboard, Stephen enjoys reading and experiencing world cuisine.

LOBSTER STOCK

3 (5 to 6-ounce) (150-170 g) Maine lobster tails
1 tablespoon (15 g) unsalted butter
1 shallot, finely diced
1 small yellow onion, finely diced
1 clove garlic, chopped
Shells of the lobster tails
1/4 cup (60 ml) brandy
1 large tomato, peeled, seeded and diced
1 tablespoon (15 g) tomato paste
2 tablespoons (30 g) all-purpose flour
3/4 cup (175 ml) fish stock, warmed (page 158)
1 teaspoon (5 g) chopped tarragon
1/4 teaspoon (1.2 g) chopped thyme
Salt and freshly ground black pepper

LOBSTER SAUCE

1 tablespoon (15 g) butter
12 pieces large shrimp, raw, peeled and deveined
1/3 cup (90 ml) dry white wine
Salt and freshly ground white pepper
1/3 bunch basil, julienned
1/3 cup (90 ml) heavy cream, loosely whipped

PASTA

1 pound (450 g) dry spaghetti pasta
1 teaspoon (5 ml) extra virgin olive oil

VEGETABLES

1/3 pound (150 g) baby squash
1/3 pound (150 g) patty pan squash
1/3 cup (90 g) green peas

GARNISH

Basil leaves

SPAGHETTINI ALL'ARAGOSTA E MAZZANCOLLE

Prawns and Lobster Spaghetti in Lobster Cream Sauce

To prepare lobster stock, steam lobster tails for 5 minutes, remove and let cool. Separate meat from the shells and slice 1/2-inch (1.2 cm) thick. Set aside.

In a saucepan over medium heat, melt butter and sauté shallot and onion for 4 minutes, until translucent. Add garlic and sauté for a few seconds. Add lobster shells, stir for a few seconds and moisten with brandy. Stir in tomato and tomato paste and simmer for 5 minutes. Add flour, stirring until it has disappeared. Add fish stock a little at a time, stirring between each addition, to dissolve lumps. Add herbs and simmer for 20 to 25 minutes. Strain through a fine sieve.

For lobster sauce, in a small saucepan over medium heat, melt butter and sauté shrimp and lobster for 1 minute. Add white wine, season with salt and pepper, add lobster stock and simmer for 5 minutes. Do not boil.

Cook spaghetti in a stockpot of boiling salted water until al dente, about 6 to 8 minutes. Drain well and toss with olive oil.

Blanch vegetables for 2 minutes, then cool in ice water and drain well. Set aside.

At the last minute, stir basil and cream into sauce to create a froth and gently toss pasta with sauce.

Serve on warmed plates and garnish with basil leaves.

Serves 4.

CULINARY NOTES:

Lobsters are best if purchased while they are still alive. A live lobster should have a hard, dark-red or black shell and display a lot of movement both in and out of the water. Lobsters curl their tails under their body when picked up.

Lobsters should be prepared immediately but will keep fresh in the refrigerator for 2 days if wrapped in damp newspaper punched with holes.

Shrimp are customarily packaged for sale based on count or the number of individual headless, shell-on shrimp in a pound. "10 and under" means ten or less shrimp per pound, "10-15" yields between 10 and 15 shrimp per pound. You should not purchase shrimp by their names, e.g. jumbo, large or medium.

Fish & Seafood

FRUIT SALSA

3 firm mangoes, peeled and julienned

1 firm small papaya, peeled and julienned

2 pink grapefruits, segmented and halved lengthwise

2 oranges, peeled and segmented (reserve orange ribs for citrus butter)

2 limes, peeled and segmented

Juice of 1 orange

Juice of 1 lime

¼ bunch chives, finely chopped

¼ bunch cilantro leaves

FISH

½ cup (120 g) Japanese breadcrumbs

½ bunch parsley, finely chopped

¼ bunch thyme, finely chopped

6 (6-ounce) (170 g) Alaskan halibut steaks

Juice of 1 lemon

Salt and freshly ground black pepper

2 tablespoons (30 ml) extra virgin olive oil

6 cedar planks, purchased

POTATOES

15 small red creamer potatoes, cut in half

2 tablespoons (30 ml) extra virgin olive oil

Salt and freshly ground black pepper

SPICED CITRUS BUTTER

¼ cup (60 g) sugar

¼ cup (60 ml) water

Juice of 2 oranges

Juice of ½ lemon

¼ teaspoon (1 g) sambal oelek

¼ cup (60 g) unsalted butter

GARNISH

6 limes, halved and grilled

BROILED ALASKAN HALIBUT ON CEDAR PLANKS

WINE PAIRING – CHARDONNAY, JORDAN, RUSSIAN RIVER, CALIFORNIA

Preheat oven to 325°F or 165°C.

For salsa, mix all ingredients except herbs in a stainless steel bowl, cover and refrigerate.

For halibut, mix breadcrumbs and herbs into a stainless steel container.

Pat dry halibut steaks, drizzle with lemon juice and season with salt and pepper. Carefully dip each steak into breadcrumb mixture. Arrange halibut steaks on cedar planks, drizzle with olive oil and bake for 15 minutes.

Blanch potatoes in boiling salted water for 8 minutes. Cool in ice water, drain and set aside. In a sauté pan, over medium high heat, warm olive oil and sauté potatoes for 5 minutes or until golden. Season with salt and pepper. Keep warm.

For citrus butter, melt sugar with water in a small saucepan over medium heat and caramelize until golden brown. Remove from heat, add citrus juices and orange ribs and simmer for 10 minutes. Strain through a sieve and transfer into a small saucepan; add sambal oelek and simmer for 5 minutes or until sauce coats the back of a wooden spoon. Remove from heat and whisk in butter a little at a time.

Remove fruit salsa from fridge and mix with fresh herbs.

Serve fish on the plank garnished with grilled lime and sautéed potatoes. Spoon fruit salsa and citrus butter in individual side dishes for all to enjoy as an accompaniment.

Serves 6.

CULINARY NOTES:

Cooking on cedar planks is a great way to infuse a smoky flavor into fish or other items. You are now able to find cedar planks specifically for broiling and/or grilling. Cedar planks can be somewhat expensive and don't last very long. (After all, you are setting them on fire.) You may be able to find bundles of untreated cedar shingles or shims at your local hardware store that will work just as well. Just make sure they are untreated! While grilling, keep a spray bottle filled with water handy and keep an eye on the plank. If it catches fire just spray it out.

LENTILS
2 tablespoons (30 ml) extra virgin olive oil
1 medium yellow onion, cut into small cubes
2 carrots cut into small cubes
8-ounces (225g) brown French lentils,
washed and soaked in cold water for 3 hours
1/4 cup Verjus wine
2 cups (480 ml) chicken stock (page 158)
3 tablespoons (45 ml) clam juice, store bought
Salt and freshly ground black pepper

VERJUS BEURRE BLANC
1 teaspoon (5 ml) extra virgin olive oil
2 shallots, minced

1 small yellow onion, diced
1/4 cup (60 ml) Verjus wine
3/4 cup (175 ml) fish stock (page 158)
1/4 cup (60 ml) heavy cream
1/4 teaspoon (1 g) saffron
3/4 pound (340 g) cold, cubed unsalted butter
Salt and freshly ground white pepper

VEGETABLES
1/2 pound (250 g) green beans
1/2 pound (250 g) snow peas, stems removed
8-ounces (225 g) grape tomatoes,
halved lengthwise

1 tablespoon (15 ml) extra virgin olive oil
Salt and freshly ground black pepper

SALMON
6 (6-ounce or 170 g) salmon fillets, skin on
Salt and freshly ground black pepper
3 tablespoons (45 g) corn flour
3 tablespoons (45 ml) extra virgin olive oil

GARNISH
2 tablespoons (30 ml) extra virgin olive oil
1 teaspoon (5 g) butter
1 small white onion, sliced into fine rings

SALMON AND VERJUS BEURRE BLANC

WINE PAIRING – 🍷 – CHARDONNAY, PETALUMA WINERY, ADELAIDE HILLS, AUSTRALIA

Preheat oven to 350°F or 180°C.

For lentils, in a large saucepan or medium stockpot, warm oil over medium heat and sauté onions and carrots for 4 minutes or until onions are translucent. Add drained lentils and deglaze with Verjus wine. Add chicken stock and clam juice. Adjust seasoning with salt and pepper and simmer, uncovered for 30 minutes or until lentils are tender. Keep warm.

To prepare Verjus beurre blanc, in a saucepan over medium heat, warm oil and sauté shallots and onion for 4 minutes. Do not brown. Deglaze with Verjus wine. Add fish stock, bring to a simmer and slowly reduce liquid by half. Add cream and saffron and simmer for 10 minutes or until sauce coats the back of a wooden spoon. Do not boil. Blend and strain through a fine sieve and whisk in cold butter a little at a time. Season with salt and pepper. Set aside and keep warm.

Blanch green beans in boiling salted water for 5 minutes and snow peas for 2 minutes. Remove from water and immediately plunge into ice water. Drain and reserve.

Season salmon fillets with salt and pepper. Brush salmon skin with oil and dust with corn flour.

In a sauté pan over high heat warm olive oil and sear salmon for 1 minute on each side. Arrange on a lightly oiled sheet pan or roasting pan and bake in the oven for 12 to 15 minutes based on desired doneness.

Meanwhile in a small sauté pan, over medium heat, warm oil and butter and sauté onion rings for 3 minutes or until golden.

Reheat green vegetables by plunging them in boiling water for 2 minutes. Drain well and sauté in a small saucepan

over medium heat in warmed oil for 2 minutes. Remove to side, reheat pan and lightly sauté the tomato halves. Season all vegetables with salt and pepper.

Place lentils in the center of warmed plate and top with snow peas and green beans, sautéed tomatoes and salmon fillet. Spoon some beurre blanc around fish and vegetables and top with onion rings.

Serves 6.

CULINARY NOTES:

Verjus, (or Green Juice), is made by pressing unripe grapes. It has a pronounced sour flavor and is commonly used in dressings and sauces where a certain amount of acidity is desired. Typically verjus will be used in a dish where wine is going to be served as the verjus provides a sour taste without competing with the taste of the wine the way lemon juice or vinegar would.

ONION CONFIT
½ head of garlic, peeled and shaved
2 medium onions, peeled and shaved
⅓ cup (90 ml) extra virgin olive oil

CRAB MASH
2 pounds (1 kg) Red bliss or Baby red potatoes, peeled and halved
2 teaspoons (10 g) butter
1 shallot, finely diced
6-ounce (180 g) crab meat
3 tablespoons (45 ml) dry white wine
⅓ cup (90 ml) sour cream
2 tablespoons (30 g) chopped chives

SHRIMP
18 extra large size shrimp, peeled, deveined and tails left on (size U5)

BEURRE BLANC
1 shallot, minced
3 tablespoons (45 ml) brandy
¾ cup (175 ml) fish stock (page 158)
½ pound (250 g) cubed, unsalted cold butter
Salt and freshly ground black pepper

SAUTÉED MUSHROOMS
6-ounces (150 g) baby portabella mushrooms, quartered
Salt and freshly ground black pepper
1 tablespoon (15 g) minced fresh parsley

SAUTÉED SPINACH
½ pound (250 g) fresh spinach, stems off
Salt and freshly ground black pepper

GARNISH
Chive sprigs
3 lemons, halved and grilled
1 tomato, seeded and small diced

GRILLED JUMBO SHRIMP

WINE PAIRING – SAUVIGNON BLANC, BARONS DE ROTHSCHILD · LAFITE, BORDEAUX, "RÉSERVE SPÉCIALE," FRANCE

In a small saucepan over medium heat, simmer garlic and onion in olive oil for 20 minutes. Do not brown. Allow to cool. Cover and reserve.

To prepare crab mash, place potatoes in salted cold water, bring to a boil and cook until potatoes are easily pierced with the tip of a knife, about 20 minutes. Drain and press potatoes through a potato ricer into a heated bowl. If a potato ricer is not available use a stand mixer and wire whisk attachment. Whip potatoes until smooth and creamy.

In a small sauté pan over medium heat, melt butter and sauté shallots for 2 minutes. Do not brown. Add crab meat and 2 tablespoons (30 ml) onion confit, season with salt and pepper and deglaze with wine.

Fold crab mixture into potatoes. Add sour cream and chives and adjust seasoning with salt and pepper. Keep warm.

Brush shrimp with 3 tablespoons (45 ml) onion confit. Lightly oil a grill pan and heat over medium-high heat. Place shrimp on grill and cook each side for 3 to 4 minutes, turning only once. Season with salt and pepper. Remove shrimp from pan and keep warm.

To make beurre blanc, return pan to medium heat, warm 1 tablespoon (15 ml) confit and sauté shallots for 2 minutes. Deglaze pan with brandy, add fish stock and reduce by half. Remove from heat and whisk in butter a little at a time. Strain through a sieve. Adjust seasoning with salt and pepper.

For mushrooms, in a sauté pan over medium heat, warm 2 tablespoons (30 ml) of onion confit and sauté mushrooms and parsley for 5 minutes. Season with salt and pepper.

For spinach, in a saucepan over medium heat, warm 2 tablespoons (30 ml) of onion confit and sauté spinach for 2 minutes. Season with salt and pepper. Drain excess water.

Arrange crab mash off centered in warmed plates and top with shrimp. Place mushrooms and spinach on plates and surround with shrimp sauce. Garnish with chive sprigs, grilled lemon and diced tomato.

Serves 6.

CULINARY NOTES:

Making a Beurre Blanc, or Butter Sauce, is not complicated at all. Essentially you are trying to combine 2 unlike ingredients together to create an emulsion. The trick is to use cubes of cold butter added slowly to the hot sauce and whisking until the ingredients combine. If the finished sauce separates or "breaks," return it to the heat, slowly warm the sauce and add another small amount of cold butter.

ONION CONFIT

½ head of garlic, peeled and shaved
2 medium onions, peeled and shaved
⅓ cup (90 ml) extra virgin olive oil

VEGETABLES

2 tablespoons (30 ml) extra virgin olive oil
1 medium yellow onion, chopped
2 cloves garlic, finely shaved
1 6-ounce (170 g) can Italian tomatoes, diced
6 new potatoes, peeled, diced and lightly pan-fried
3 plum tomatoes, peeled, seeded and diced
18 black olives, pitted and halved
1 cauliflower, cut in small florettes, blanched and
tossed in onion confit

2 tablespoons (30 g) chopped Italian parsley
1 teaspoon (15 g) fresh thyme leaves
Salt and freshly ground black pepper

WARM SHRIMP SALSA

2 teaspoons (10 ml) extra virgin olive oil
1 tablespoon (15 ml) clarified butter
1 small white onion, diced
½ cup (115 g) baby shrimp
2 plum tomatoes, peeled, seeded and diced
1 tablespoon (15 g) chopped parsley
1 teaspoon (5 g) fresh thyme
1 teaspoon (5 g) lemon zest
Salt and freshly ground white pepper

FISH

12 (3-ounce) (85 g) Pangasius (Basa) fish fillets
or catfish
¼ cup (60 ml) extra virgin olive oil
Salt and freshly ground white pepper

GREEN BEANS

½ pound green beans, blanched
2 tablespoons (30 g) butter
Salt and freshly ground white pepper

GARNISH

12 caper berries

MEDITERRANEAN PANGASIUS FISH FILLETS

WINE PAIRING – ♟ – PINOT GRIGIO, DANZANTE, VENEZIE, ITALY

Preheat oven to 350°F or 175°C.

For the onion confit, in a small saucepan over medium heat, simmer garlic and onion in olive oil for 20 minutes. Do not brown. Allow to cool. Cover and reserve.

For vegetables, in a large sauté pan or wok, over low heat, warm oil and sauté onion and garlic for 5 minutes. Add canned tomatoes and slowly cook until thick. Toss in fried potatoes, fresh tomatoes, olives and cauliflower. Season with salt and pepper. Stir well and cook for 10 minutes. When ready to serve, toss in fresh herbs.

To make shrimp salsa, in a small sauté pan over medium heat, warm oil and butter together and sauté onion for 3 minutes or until translucent. Add shrimp and tomatoes and sauté for 3 to 5 minutes. Incorporate remaining ingredients and season to taste. Mix well and keep warm.

Season fish with salt and pepper. In a sauté pan over high heat, warm oil and sear fish for 1 minute on each side. Arrange on a sheet pan and finish in the oven for 5 to 7 minutes.

Reheat green beans by dipping them into boiling water for 2 to 3 minutes. In a small saucepan over medium heat, melt butter and sauté green beans for 5 minutes or until warmed throughout. Season with salt and pepper.

To serve, arrange vegetables in the center of warmed plates. Stack with 2 pieces of fish and finish with shrimp salsa. Garnish with caper berries and place green beans sideways on the plates.

Serves 6.

RATATOUILLE

3 tablespoons (45 ml) extra virgin olive oil

1 small (2.5 inches or 6 cm) gingerroot, peeled and crushed

2 cloves garlic, thinly sliced

2 small white onions, diced

2 small eggplants, diced

1 red bell pepper, diced

1 green bell pepper, diced

1 yellow bell pepper, diced

1/3 pound (150 g) shiitake mushrooms, cut in half

2 small zucchini, diced

2 plum tomatoes, diced

1 6-ounce (170 g) can tomato strips

1/8 bunch basil, julienned

1/8 bunch cilantro, chopped

2 tablespoons (30 ml) rice vinegar

Salt and freshly ground black pepper

AIOLI

3 tablespoons (45 ml) rice vinegar

1 egg yolk

1 teaspoon (5 g) Dijon mustard

1 clove garlic, minced

Salt and freshly ground white pepper

1 cup (250 ml) olive oil

1/4 teaspoon (1 g) wasabi powder

1/4 teaspoon (1 ml) soy sauce

1 teaspoon (5 ml) mirin wine

FISH

6 (6 to 7-ounce) (170 to 200 g) tilapia fillets

1/4 cup (60 g) cornmeal

Salt and freshly ground white pepper

GARNISH

3 lemons, halved

Parsley sprigs

CORNMEAL DUSTED TILAPIA

WINE PAIRING – ♟ – BODEGAS JULIÁN CHIVITE, ROSADO, NAVARRA, "GRAN FEUDO," SPAIN

Preheat oven to 350°F or 180°C.

For the ratatouille, in a large sauté pan or wok, over medium heat, warm olive oil and sauté ginger, garlic and onion for 5 minutes. Set aside. Sauté each vegetable type separately for 3 minutes in hot oil. Combine all vegetables into the sauté pan or wok; add fresh and canned tomatoes and season with salt and pepper. Stir well. Add basil, cilantro and rice vinegar and simmer for 20 minutes or until vegetables are cooked. Keep warm.

For aioli, place 3/4 of the rice vinegar, egg yolk, mustard, garlic, salt and pepper in a small glass bowl. While beating mixture, slowly drizzle in oil. Incorporate wasabi, soy sauce, mirin and remaining vinegar.

Stir well. Adjust seasoning, cover and refrigerate until ready to use.

Season tilapia fillets with salt and pepper and dust top side with cornmeal.

Sear fish on both sides, dusted side first, on a hot griddle lightly oiled. Transfer into a baking pan and bake for 5 minutes.

Serve ratatouille and tilapia fillets on warmed plates. Spoon some aioli over fish and garnish with lemon and parsley sprig.

Serve with a side dish of aioli.

Roasted potato wedges would be a great accompaniment to the dish.

Serves 6.

CULINARY NOTES:

Probably the single most important piece of equipment in the kitchen is a good set of sharp knives. Hundreds of sizes and styles are available and there are knives designed for specific tasks. What brand, style or type you use depends on your personal preference and what you are planning to do. Remember, a dull knife is much more dangerous than a sharp one! If you use a dull knife you have to exert more pressure and the blade can twist or slip. Always keep your knives as sharp as possible. Investing in a quality sharpener is a great idea. If you are uneasy about sharpening them yourself have them sharpened professionally.

GINGER CONFIT

1/3 cup (90 ml) extra virgin olive oil
2 heads fresh ginger, peeled and shaved
1/2 head of garlic, peeled and shaved

PLUM SAUCE

1/3 cup (90 ml) sweet chili sauce
1/3 cup (90 ml) plum sauce
1/4 cup (60 ml) soy sauce
Juice of 1 lime
2 tablespoons (30 g) corn starch (as needed)

VEGETABLE STIR-FRY

4 tablespoons (60 ml) ginger confit
2 carrots, peeled and sliced diagonally
1 red bell pepper, thickly sliced
1 green bell pepper, thickly sliced
1 small red onion, thickly sliced
1/4 pound (125 g) snow peas
2 baby bok choy, cut in half lengthwise
1/4 bunch cilantro, finely chopped
2 tablespoons (30 g) julienned green onions
Salt and freshly ground black pepper
4-ounces (120 g) baby spinach
2 tablespoons (30 ml) soy sauce
1 tablespoon (15 ml) sesame oil

1 tablespoon (15 g) finely chopped cilantro

FISH

1/2 cup (115 g) tempura batter, purchased
8 (2-inches) (5 cm) pieces Mahi Mahi
16 large size shrimp, peeled and deveined, tails
on, butterflied (size 16/20)
Salt and freshly ground black pepper
1/4 cup (60 g) all-purpose flour
1 cup (140 ml) vegetable oil, for frying

GARNISH

Cilantro sprigs

SHRIMP AND MAHI MAHI TEMPURA

WINE PAIRING – ￼ – RIESLING, SELBACH-OSTER, SPÄTLESE, MOSEL, GERMANY

To prepare the confit, in a saucepan over low heat, warm oil and simmer ginger and garlic for 20 minutes. Do not brown. Allow to cool. Cover and reserve.

To make the plum sauce, in a small stainless steel bowl, mix together the sweet chili sauce, plum sauce, soy sauce, lime juice and 3 tablespoons (45 ml) of ginger confit.

Transfer into a small saucepan and bring to a boil. Thicken with corn starch and strain through a fine sieve.

For the stir-fry, heat a wok or large sauté pan over low heat and warm 4 tablespoons (60 ml) of ginger confit. Toss in vegetables and sauté for 5 minutes over high heat. Season with salt and

pepper and add spinach, soy sauce and sesame oil. Sauté for another 5 minutes and set aside. Keep warm and add chopped cilantro just before serving.

For the fish and shrimp tempura, warm oil in a frying pan over medium/high heat.

Prepare tempura batter according to the instructions on the package.

Pat dry and season the Mahi Mahi and shrimp with salt and pepper.

Dredge in flour and shake off any excess.

Dip each piece into the tempura batter and deep-fry in the hot vegetable oil; 5 to 6 minutes for the Mahi Mahi and 3 minutes for the shrimp. Drain and place on paper towels.

To serve, line plates with stir-fried vegetables and top with fish and shrimp.

Garnish with cilantro sprigs and serve with a side dish of plum sauce.

Serves 8.

CULINARY NOTES:

What is confit?

Traditionally confit is a cooking method used for preserving meats by submerging them in their own rendered fat. The meat is slowly braised and allowed to cool. The fat creates an airtight seal which preserves the meat for an extended period. In this case, we use a confit to enhance the oil with the flavors of garlic and ginger and use it as a base to cook the stir-fried vegetables.

5 tablespoons (75 g) butter
2 tablespoons (30 g) chopped parsley
1 tablespoon (15 g) chopped thyme
1 tablespoon (15 g) chopped chervil

COMBO

4 (6 to 7-ounce) (170 to 200 g) lobster tails
Salt and freshly ground black pepper
1/4 cup (60 ml) extra virgin olive oil
2 cloves garlic, minced
*12 large size shrimp, peeled, deveined,
and tails left on (size 16/20)*
Juice of 1 lemon

VEGETABLES

1/2 pound (250 g) baby carrots
1 spear broccoli, cut into florets
2 tablespoons (30 g) butter

GARNISH

Dill or tarragon sprigs
2 lemons, halved

LOBSTER AND SHRIMP COMBO

WINE PAIRING – VOUVRAY, RÉMY PANNIER, LOIRE, FRANCE

Preheat oven to 450°F or 230°C.

In a small saucepan over medium heat, melt butter and stir in herbs. Keep warm.

With a sharp knife, cut lobster tail shells down the soft underside to expose the flesh. Season with salt and pepper, then brush with some of the butter-herb mixture. Broil lobsters for 6 to 8 minutes until the tail meat is white.

Blanch carrots in boiling salted water for 8 minutes. Cool in ice, drain and set aside.

Blanch broccoli in boiling salted water for 5 minutes. Cool in ice water, drain and set aside.

In a sauté pan over high heat, warm olive oil and sauté garlic and shrimp for 5 to 7 minutes, until shrimp are pink. Season with salt, pepper and lemon juice.

Reheat carrots and broccoli in hot water at the last minute for a few seconds. In a pan, over medium heat, melt butter and sauté vegetables for 3 to 4 minutes until heated through.

Using a fork, bring lobster meat out of the shell.

Serve on warmed plates surrounded by vegetables and drizzle with warm herbed butter.

Garnish with dill and lemon halves.

Serves 4.

CULINARY NOTES:

Sauté means "to jump" and is a cooking technique where small amounts of food are cooked quickly over high heat. If you need to sauté large quantities of something, it is best to do it in small batches. A large amount of items in a pan, all at once, will drive down the temperature and extend the cooking time. You will also find that a lot of water appears and the items are stewing as opposed to browning.

SALSA

1/2 pound (250 g) tomatillos, husked, rinsed, cored and chopped
1 large avocado, halved, pitted and peeled
1/2 jalapeño chili, chopped
1/4 cup (60 g) chopped fresh cilantro
1 green onion, chopped
1 cup (235 g) peeled, cored and diced pineapple
1 tablespoon (15 ml) extra virgin olive oil
Salt and freshly ground black pepper

BROWN RICE PILAF

1 tablespoon (15 g) butter
3 green onions, chopped
1 cup (235 g) Basmati light brown rice
2 tablespoons (30 ml) dry white wine
2 cups (475 ml) chicken stock, hot (page 158)
2 cups (475 ml) water, as needed

1/2 cup (120 g) pecans

2 tablespoons (30 g) butter

FISH

4 (7-ounce) (200 g) Mahi Mahi fillets
Salt and freshly group white pepper
1 tablespoon (15 ml) extra virgin olive oil

GARNISH

Cilantro sprigs
2 lemons, halved and marked on the grill

Sean MacDougall, Executive Chef, CEC

A graduate of the Royal Culinary Institute of Westminster (England) Chef Sean worked in various hotels and restaurants throughout England as well as owned his own business in Dover. His passion for food and his love of travel led him to embark on new challenges aboard cruise ships. Chef Sean worked for several cruise lines before joining Royal Caribbean International in 2007. When not onboard, he enjoys surfing, reading and going to the movies.

GRILLED MAHI MAHI AND TOMATILLO SALSA

Preheat oven to 380°F or 195°C.

For salsa place all ingredients into a food processor and blend to a coarse purée. Transfer into a stainless steel or glass bowl, season with salt and pepper, cover and refrigerate.

To make rice, in a saucepan over medium heat, melt butter and sauté onions for 1 minute. Add brown rice and continue to cook, stirring continually for 2 minutes. Deglaze with wine and add chicken stock. Bring to a boil, reduce heat and simmer for 30 to 40 minutes or until cooked through. Stir occasionally, adding water as needed.

Spread out pecans in a single layer on a baking sheet. Place in the oven and toast for 8 minutes. Do not allow to burn.

For fish, lightly oil a grill pan and heat over medium-high heat. Pat dry fish, season with salt and pepper and brush with a little olive oil. Place fillets on grill and cook each side for 3 to 4 minutes, turning only once.

Fold butter into rice with a fork. Add pecans and gently mix.

Place rice in a mound in the center of warmed plates and top with fish. Finish with a spoonful of salsa on each fillet and garnish with cilantro and grilled lemon.

Serves 4.

MARINADE

2 cloves garlic, crushed
2 teaspoons (10 ml) freshly squeezed lemon juice
1 teaspoon (5 g) ground cumin
1/2 teaspoon (2.5 g) sweet paprika
1/2 teaspoon (2.5 g) powdered saffron
1/2 teaspoon (2.5 g) peeled and ground ginger
2 tablespoons (30 g) chopped cilantro
2 tablespoons (30 g) chopped parsley
2 tablespoons (30 ml) vegetable oil
Salt and freshly ground black pepper

20 jumbo prawns, peeled and deveined
3 tablespoons (45 ml) extra virgin olive oil
Salt and freshly ground black pepper

TOMATO CHARMOULA

2 teaspoons (10 g) cumin seeds
1 teaspoon (5 g) coriander seeds
1 can (16-ounce) (450 g) whole
tomatoes, drained
2 cloves garlic, crushed
2 red chilies, seeded and finely chopped
2 tablespoons (30 g) tomato paste
Juice of 1 lemon
1 teaspoon (5 g) ground sweet paprika

COUSCOUS

1 cup (250 g) couscous
1 1/2 cups (400 ml) chicken stock, hot
1 yellow bell pepper, finely chopped
1 green bell pepper, finely chopped
2 cloves garlic, crushed
1/2 cup (120 g) chopped green olives
2/3 teaspoon (3 g) ground cumin
3 tablespoons (45 g) chopped parsley

JUMBO PRAWNS WITH MOROCCAN SPICES, TOMATO CHARMOULA AND GREEN OLIVE COUSCOUS

Prepare the marinade in a stainless steel bowl by mixing all ingredients.

Pat dry prawns and coat with marinade. Cover and refrigerate for 2 hours.

For Tomato Charmoula, place cumin and coriander seeds in a small sauté pan over high heat and dry roast for 15 seconds, until the seeds have released their fragrance. Remove from heat and finely crush. Transfer to a blender with remaining ingredients and blend for about 3 minutes, until a paste consistency is reached. Refrigerate until ready to use.

Place couscous in a bowl and moisten with stock. Cover and set aside for 6 to 8 minutes, until couscous swells. Fluff up with a spoon and cover again for 6 minutes. Fold in peppers, garlic, olives and cumin and mix well. Set aside and keep warm. Toss in parsley just before serving.

Heat a heavy skillet over high heat and warm the oil. Sauté prawns for 6 minutes, until they turn pink. Adjust the seasoning with salt and pepper.

On warmed plates, arrange the couscous and top with prawns. Serve with Tomato Charmoula on the side.

Serves 4.

*Helga B. Finnsdottir, Manager,
Newbuild, CEC, CCA*

Chef Helga joined Royal Caribbean International's fleet in August 1999 as the first female Executive Chef to be hired by RCCL. Helga hails from the land of Fire & Ice: Iceland. Her passion for cooking started at the early age of 14, when she worked in leading hotels in Iceland during summer and holiday breaks from school. She studied Provision and Dietary, followed by a 4-year apprenticeship at the Culinary School of Iceland. She has cooked for foreign dignitaries and in fine hotels in Norway and England. Helga began her career at sea in 1993 aboard the QE2. When Helga is not cooking, she enjoys being with family and friends, hiking and biking and winter sports.

PARSNIPS

5 medium parsnips, peeled and cut
1½ inch (4 cm) thick

6 cloves garlic

2 bay leaves

2 cups (500 ml) milk

2 tablespoons (30 g) butter, room temperature

MASHED POTATOES

1 pound (450 g) Idaho potatoes, peeled,
quartered

⅓ cup (90 ml) heavy cream

1 tablespoon (15 g) unsalted butter

Salt and freshly ground black pepper

CHORIZO OIL

¼ cup (60 ml) extra virgin olive oil

1 tablespoon (15 g) ground paprika

Chorizo sausage trimmings

¼ bunch chives, chopped

SCALLOPS

2 chorizo sausages, sliced ½ inch
(1.5 cm) thick at an angle

30 sea scallops

1 tablespoon (15 ml) extra virgin olive oil

Salt and freshly ground white pepper

PETITE SALAD

½ cup (120 g) assorted salad leaves such as lollo
rosso, Belgium endive and frisée lettuce

1 plum tomato, seeded and thinly cut lengthwise

Juice of 1 lemon

2 tablespoons (30 ml) extra virgin olive oil

Salt and freshly ground black pepper

SEARED DIVER SCALLOPS AND CHORIZO

WINE PAIRING – GEWURZTRAMINER, DOPFF & IRION, ALSACE, FRANCE

Place parsnips, garlic and bay leaves in milk in a heavy bottom stockpot. Bring to a boil and simmer for 15 minutes or until parsnips are tender and can easily be pierced with the tip of a fork. Strain parsnips, discarding garlic and bay leaves and reserving milk. Transfer into a food processor and blend until smooth. Add butter and enough of reserved milk to form a smooth purée.

For mashed potatoes, place potatoes into salted cold water, bring to a boil and cook until potatoes are easily pierced with the tip of a knife, about 15 minutes. Drain and press potatoes through a potato ricer into a heated bowl. Stir in cream and butter. Incorporate parsnip purée and mix well. Adjust seasoning with salt and pepper. Set aside and keep warm.

For chorizo oil, in a small saucepan over medium heat, warm oil and paprika and sauté chorizo trimmings for 3 minutes. Let cool and strain. Add chives before serving.

In a small frying pan over medium to high heat, warm half of the olive oil and fry chorizo slices on both sides. Remove from the pan and keep warm.

Rinse pan and return to high heat. Pat dry and season scallops with salt and pepper. Warm remaining oil and sear scallops for 2 minutes on each side, in batches over medium to high heat. Set aside.

To make petite salad, toss salad leaves and tomatoes with lemon juice and olive oil until moist. Season to taste.

To serve, place a spoonful of vegetable purée in the center of warm plates. Arrange scallops and chorizo on top and garnish with the petite salad.

Crown with drops of chorizo oil.

Serves 6.

CULINARY NOTES:

Chorizo sausage is a Spanish sausage made with a mixture of ground pork, pepper and chilies. Chorizo is readily available in most supermarkets but equal substitutions can be made with Andouille, Abruzzo, or Italian Sweet Sausage.

Of the 400 species of scallops available on the open market, sea scallops, bay scallops and calico scallops are the most popular. In the Unites States, bay scallops are favored over sea and calico scallops, as they tend to have a sweeter flavor. Calico scallops have to be steamed open to release the muscle from the shell, thus they arrive to market fully cooked, which makes them less desirable. Sea scallops are much larger and have a more "meaty" quality.

VEGETABLE SALSA

1 yellow bell pepper
4 tablespoons (60 ml) extra virgin olive oil
1 medium red onion, finely diced
2 cloves garlic, chopped
1 zucchini, finely diced
1 fennel, finely diced
1 eggplant, finely diced
2 tomatoes, peeled, seeded and diced
2 tablespoons (30 g) chopped basil
1 tablespoon (15 g) chopped parsley
Salt and freshly ground black pepper

BOUILLABAISSE SAUCE

2 tablespoons (30 ml) extra virgin olive oil
2 leeks, white part only, chopped
1 fennel bulb, chopped
1 clove garlic, chopped
1/2 teaspoon (2 g) saffron
1 tablespoon (15 g) chopped oregano
1/4 teaspoon (1 g) fennel seeds
2 tablespoons (30 ml) Anisette liqueur
4 plum tomatoes, peeled and seeded
1 cup (250 ml) fish stock (page 158)
Salt and freshly ground black pepper

TUNA

2 pounds (1 kg) ahi tuna fillets
2 tablespoons (30 g) tahini paste
3 tablespoons (45 g) black sesame seeds
3 tablespoons (45 g) white sesame seeds
1 tablespoon (15 ml) extra virgin olive oil
1 tablespoon (15 ml) sesame oil
Salt and freshly ground black pepper

GARNISH

1/4 teaspoon (1 g) white sesame seeds
1/4 teaspoon (1 g) black sesame seeds

Thomas Pellocheck, Executive Chef, CEC

Chef Thomas joined Royal Caribbean International in
1998. Born in Frankfurt, Germany, he studied for
3 years in Germany and 2 years in Switzerland. After
graduation, Thomas worked in Frankfurt as a Sous
Chef for 4 years, then moved to Cairo to work as an
Executive Chef for the Sheraton and Intercontinental
Hotel chains. During this time, Thomas traveled
to Turkey, Russia, Argentina and then to Munich,
Germany, to join the Kempinski Hotel Four Seasons. In
his spare time Thomas enjoys reading and gardening.

MEDITERRANEAN TUNA

Preheat oven to 350°F or 180°C.

For salsa, place pepper in an ovenproof
dish and drizzle with 2 tablespoons of
olive oil. Roast for 20 minutes or until
brown and blistery. Remove pepper from
oven and place in a small bowl. Cover with
plastic wrap. A small, tightly closed paper
bag will do also. This loosens the skins
and eases peeling. Finely dice the pepper.

In a sauté pan over medium heat warm
the remaining oil and sauté the onion
and garlic for 5 minutes, until translucent
and fragrant. Add vegetables, season with
salt and pepper and sauté for 5 minutes.
Adjust seasoning, remove from heat and
add herbs and pepper. Mix well, cover and
refrigerate for 1 hour.

For sauce, in a saucepan over medium
heat, warm oil and sauté leeks, fennel and
garlic for 3 minutes, until fragrant. Do not
brown. Add saffron, oregano and fennel
seeds and stir for 30 seconds. Deglaze

with the Anisette liqueur. Add tomatoes
and stir for 1 minute. Add fish stock and
simmer for 20 minutes. Remove from heat
and let cool. Adjust seasoning with salt
and pepper. Transfer to a blender and
blend for 5 minutes, until smooth. Strain
through a sieve and set aside. Keep warm.

Coat tuna with tahini paste. Spread
sesame seeds on a plate and press tuna
firmly onto them on all sides. Heat olive
oil and sesame oil in a nonstick skillet
over medium high heat. Add tuna, season
with salt and pepper and cook until done
rare, for 2 minutes on each side or until
desired doneness. Remove from heat and
cut crosswise into 1/3-inch-thick slices
(0.8 cm).

Spoon sauce onto serving plates and
fan tuna slices over sauce. Sprinkle with
sesame seeds and serve salsa on the side.

Serves 4.

¹/4 cup (60 g) butter
6 shallots, minced
2 cloves garlic, minced
6 pounds (3 kg) mussels, cleaned and beards
removed (5 to 6 dozen)
3 tablespoons (45 g) flour
2 tablespoons (30 ml) Pernod®
1 cup (235 ml) dry white wine
¹/2 teaspoon (2 g) salt
¹/4 teaspoon (1 g) freshly ground pepper
2 tablespoons (30 g) chopped parsley

FRIES

Vegetable oil as needed
6 medium potatoes, peeled and cut in
¹/4 inch (0.6 cm) strips
2 medium sweet potatoes, peeled and
cut in ¹/4 inch (0.6 cm) strips
Salt

GARNISH

Parsley sprigs

MUSSELS MARINIÈRE

In a large saucepan or medium size stockpot, over medium-high heat, melt butter and sauté shallots and garlic for 3 minutes or until transparent, stirring constantly.

Add mussels and flour and mix well. Deglaze with Pernod. Add wine, salt and freshly ground pepper. Cover and simmer 6 to 8 minutes or until shells open, stirring occasionally. Finish with chopped parsley.

In a deep-fat fryer or medium size frying pan, heat about 2 inches (5 cm) of vegetable oil to 400°F or 200°C.

Rinse potato strips in cold water, drain and pat dry with a paper towel.

Gently place an even layer of strips into the hot oil and fry for 7 minutes or until golden brown. Drain on paper towels. Repeat with remaining potatoes. Sprinkle lightly with salt.

Using a ladle, transfer mussels and sauce into heated bowls, discarding any that remained unopened. Garnish each bowl with parsley sprigs.

Serve fries in separate plates.

Serves 8.

Kenneth Johansen, Executive Chef, CEC

Chef Kenneth was born in Haslev, Denmark and began his culinary career with an apprenticeship with SAS/Radisson Hotel, Copenhagen. His first onboard experience was on QE2 in 1996 where he worked as Chef de Partie before joining Royal Caribbean International in 2003 after working for various hotels and restaurants throughout Europe. While on vacation he enjoys traveling, surfing, fine wines and cuisine from around the world.

Meat & Poultry

LAMB SHANKS

6 (7-ounce) (200 g) lamb shanks, bone in
1/3 cup (90 ml) extra virgin olive oil
1/2 cup (120 g) chopped celery
2 onions, chopped
3 medium carrots, chopped
1/4 cup (60 g) tomato paste
1/3 cup (90 ml) red wine
1/4 cup (60 ml) port wine
3 cups (700 ml) demi-glace (page 159)
1 tablespoon (15 g) chopped thyme
1 tablespoon (15 g) chopped rosemary
1 teaspoon (5 g) whole black peppercorns
1 teaspoon (5 g) juniper berries

2 bay leaves
Salt and freshly ground black pepper

VEGETABLES

1/2 pound (250 g) carrots, cut into large dice
1/2 pound (250 g) celery, cut into large dice
1/2 pound (250 g) celery root, cut into large dice
1/2 pound (250 g) shallots, halved
1/3 cup (90 ml) extra virgin olive oil
2 tablespoons (30 g) chopped thyme
2 tablespoons (30 g) chopped rosemary
Salt and freshly ground black pepper

MASHED POTATOES

2 pounds (1 kg) Idaho potatoes, peeled
3/4 cup (175 ml) heavy cream
2 tablespoons (30 g) unsalted butter
Nutmeg
Salt and freshly ground black pepper

GARNISH

Rosemary and thyme sprigs

BRAISED LAMB SHANKS

WINE PAIRING –  – MALBEC, NAVARRO CORREAS, COLECCION PRIVADA, MAIPU VALLEY, ARGENTINA

Preheat oven to 375°F or 190°C.

Season shanks with salt and pepper. Heat a Dutch oven or heavy stockpot over medium-high heat for 3 to 4 minutes. Add oil and, when it is hot, add lamb shanks in batches. Sear, turning them occasionally until they are well browned on all sides, about 10 minutes. Remove shanks and set aside.

To the same Dutch oven add celery, onion and carrot. Sauté for 5 minutes or until golden brown. Add tomato paste and mix well. Add wine and port, turn up the heat to medium and reduce by half.

Add the demi-glace, herbs and seasonings and simmer for 10 minutes.

Nestle lamb shanks among vegetables in Dutch oven, making sure that they are covered in liquid. Cover and place in oven. Cook for about 1 1/2 hours, turning occasionally, until meat is falling off the bone. Remove shanks from pot and strain sauce through a cheese cloth. Season to taste with salt and pepper.

Reduce oven heat to 350°F or 180°C.

Place root vegetables in a shallow roasting pan and coat with olive oil, thyme, rosemary, salt and pepper. Roast approximately 45 minutes, until tender.

Place potatoes into salted cold water, bring to a boil and cook until potatoes are easily pierced with the tip of a knife, about 15 minutes. Drain and press potatoes through a potato ricer into a heated bowl. Stir in cream, butter and nutmeg. Adjust seasoning with salt and pepper and keep warm.

Serve each lamb shank in warmed dishes, accompanied by mashed potatoes and roasted vegetables. Spoon sauce over lamb shanks and garnish with fresh herbs.

Serves 6.

CULINARY NOTES:

Braising is a "moist heat" method of cooking tough cuts of meat. Unlike roasting or broiling (dry heat), braising relies on moisture, time and an acid to break down the tough collagen fibers. Acids like tomatoes or wine help tenderize the meat while adding flavor to the finished sauce or gravy. Stewing and pot-roasting are all forms of braising.

Roasting and broiling use a direct heat source and no moisture or acid. The only difference between roasting and baking is that baking does not use an open flame.

RAGÙ

1/2 cup (120 ml) heavy cream
2 tablespoons (30 g) extra virgin olive oil
1 medium yellow onion, chopped
2 shallots, chopped
6-ounces (170 g) button mushrooms, sliced
6-ounces (170 g) oyster mushrooms, sliced
1/4 cup (60 ml) dry white wine
2 tablespoons (30 g) chopped chives
Salt and freshly ground black pepper

MEDALLIONS

3 pork filets, trimmed and cut into 3-ounce or
85 g medallions (2 medallions per guest)
3 tablespoons (45 g) all-purpose flour
1 tablespoon (15 ml) extra virgin olive oil

1/4 cup (60 ml) extra virgin olive oil
3 medium yellow onions, diced
2 stalks celery, diced
1 bay leaf
1/4 cup (60 ml) Merlot wine
1/2 cup (120 ml) veal demi-glace (page 159)
Salt and freshly ground black pepper

VEGETABLES

2 tablespoons (30 g) butter
1 medium onion, cut into small cubes
1 bunch broccolini, trimmed or
1 head broccoli, cut into florets,
steamed and shocked in ice water
Salt and freshly ground black pepper

PORK MEDALLIONS

WINE PAIRING - ♟ - PINOT NOIR, GIANT STEPS, YARRA, AUSTRALIA

Preheat oven to 400°F or 205°C.

To prepare ragù, in a small saucepan over low heat, simmer heavy cream until it has reduced by half.

In a separate sauté pan over medium heat, warm oil and sauté onion and shallots for 3 minutes or until onions are translucent. Add mushrooms and sauté for 2 minutes. Deglaze with white wine and add reduced cream. Simmer for 2 minutes and add chopped chives. Season with salt and pepper.

Dip each pork medallion into flour, shake to eliminate excess.

In a sauté pan over medium high heat, warm oil and sear medallions on each side for 2 minutes, turning only once. Season with salt and pepper. Transfer medallions into a lightly oiled sheet pan and finish cooking in the oven for 6 minutes.

Using the same pan, sauté onions for 6 to 8 minutes or until onions are soft. Add celery and bay leaf and sauté for 3 minutes. Deglaze with Merlot wine and add demi-glace. Reduce heat and simmer for 8 minutes. Strain through a fine sieve or China Cap and adjust seasoning with salt and pepper. Keep warm on the side of the stove.

For broccolini, in a large sauté pan over medium heat, melt butter and sauté for 3 minutes, or until warm. Season with salt and pepper

Divide ragù into warmed dinner plate and top with pork medallions. Garnish with broccolini and finish with spoonful of sauce.

Serves 6.

CULINARY NOTES:

Demi-glace sauce is a rich brown sauce made from reduced veal stock and Sauce Espagnole. The time and effort required to roast the veal bones, create the stock, make the roux and reduce the sauce again, results in a wonderfully rich and flavorful sauce that is the foundation for many classical as well as contemporary dishes. Many will find, however that the investment may not be practical. Think about this though: demi-glace will keep up to six months in the refrigerator and almost indefinitely frozen. Pour the cooled sauce into ice cube trays, cover and freeze. When you need a few ounces pop out a cube or two. Your efforts will be well rewarded.

MARINADE

1 onion, julienned
2 cloves garlic, chopped
1 tablespoon chopped Scotch Bonnet pepper
1 tablespoon chopped cilantro
2 tablespoons chopped chives
1 tablespoon ketchup
1 tablespoon Worcestershire sauce
1 tablespoon Angostura® Bitters
$1/4$ teaspoon salt
Juice of 1 lemon

CHICKEN

1 ($1 1/2$ pounds) whole chicken, skinned, boned and cut into 2-inch pieces
1 tablespoon coconut oil
2 tablespoons brown sugar
1 tablespoon dark rum
1 (13.5 fl. oz.) can coconut milk
$1/2$ cup chicken stock (page 158)
Salt and freshly ground black pepper

RICE

1 cup water
1 (13.5 fl. oz.) can coconut milk
1 cup rice
$1/2$ teaspoon salt
1 onion, finely chopped
1 clove garlic, finely chopped
1 thyme sprig
1 can pigeon peas, washed and drained

GARNISH

1 cup vegetable oil
1 large ripe plantain, peeled and thinly sliced lengthwise

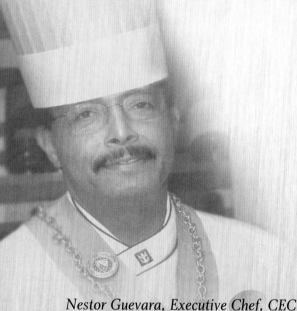

Nestor Guevara, Executive Chef, CEC

Chef Nestor comes to us from the beautiful island of Trinidad. He received one of the few scholarships offered by the Hilton School of Culinary Arts. After graduation, he spent the next 5 years employed with the Hilton Corporation, then was offered a position with one of the leading restaurant chains in America. Nestor joined the Royal Caribbean International family in 1992. He is a proud member of the Chaîne des Rôtisseurs and is also a Certified Executive Chef of the American Culinary Federation. Nestor has prepared banquets for such dignitaries as the King of Norway and members of the Chaîne des Rôtisseurs. In his spare time he enjoys cycling, European football, swimming, tennis and driving through the North American continent.

CHICKEN STEW TRINIDAD-STYLE WITH RICE AND PIGEON PEAS

For marinade, combine all ingredients into a stainless steel bowl and mix well. Coat chicken pieces, cover and refrigerate for 3 hours.

Heat a skillet over medium heat and warm oil. Add sugar and simmer until golden brown. Add chicken and sauté until chicken is coated with caramel. Deglaze with rum. Add coconut milk and chicken stock and simmer for 10 to 15 minutes or until juices run clear when pierced with a thin skewer. Adjust seasoning with salt and pepper and keep warm.

For rice, bring water and coconut milk to a boil in a small stockpot over high heat. Add the remaining ingredients except the pigeon peas and boil for 10 minutes. Add pigeon peas and simmer for another 10 minutes or until rice is cooked.

Warm oil in a skillet over high heat. Fry plantain slices for 1 minute or until golden brown. Drain and place on paper towels.

To serve, place rice in the center of warm plates and top with chicken stew. Garnish with 2 plantain chips.

BARLEY RISOTTO

2 teaspoons (10 g) butter
1 leek, white part only, finely chopped
2 carrots, peeled and finely chopped
1 cup (230 g) pearl barley, washed
1 bay leaf
4 cups (930 ml) chicken stock, warmed (page 158)
3 tablespoons (45 ml) heavy cream
2 tablespoons grated Parmesan cheese

GLAZE

2 teaspoons (10 ml) vegetable oil
2 cups (475 ml) lamb or beef stock (page 159)
3 tablespoons (45 ml) port
1 tablespoon (15 g) red currant jelly
1 tablespoon (15 g) fresh thyme sprigs

LAMB

2 6-bone rack of Saltmarsh lamb, trimmed and Frenched
Salt and freshly ground black pepper
2 tablespoons (30 ml) vegetable oil

GLAZED CARROTS

4-ounces (120 g) baby carrots
2 tablespoons (30 g) butter
2 tablespoons (30 g) sugar
1 teaspoon (5 g) fresh thyme leaves

ASPARAGUS

1 tablespoon (15 g) butter
12 green asparagus, peeled and blanched

GARNISH

Thyme sprigs

RACK OF SCOTTISH SALTMARSH LAMB WITH PEARL BARLEY RISOTTO AND BABY VEGETABLES

Preheat oven to 450°F or 230°C.

In a stockpot over medium heat, melt butter and sauté leek and carrots for 3 minutes. Add pearl barley and bay leaf and cook for 2 minutes. Add 2 cups of chicken stock and bring mixture to a boil. Reduce heat and simmer until liquid is almost absorbed, stirring frequently. Add remaining stock $1/2$ cup at a time until barley is tender (about 40 minutes). Stir in cream and Parmesan cheese and keep warm.

For glaze, in a small saucepan over medium heat, combine all ingredients, bring to a boil and simmer for 15 minutes or until the mixture has reached a glaze consistency.

Season lamb racks with salt and pepper. Heat oil in a large skillet over high heat and sear racks on both sides for 2 minutes making sure that the lamb is placed lamb bone-side down in the skillet for roasting. Cover the ends of the bones with aluminum foil to prevent charring.

Baste lamb with glaze and roast for 18 to 25 minutes depending on the degree of doneness required (20 minutes for a medium cooked lamb).

Remove from oven and let rest, loosely covered for 5 minutes before carving.

Boil carrots in salted water for 15 minutes or until tender. Drain carrots and set aside.

In a small sauté pan over medium heat, melt butter and sugar. Add carrots and cook for 5 minutes or until carrots are slightly browned and glazed. Add thyme and keep warm.

In a sauté pan over medium heat, melt butter and sauté asparagus for 5 minutes or until warmed through. Season with salt and pepper

Position barley on warmed plate and gently place lamb on top, making sure that lamb bones are upright. Garnish with thyme sprigs.

Serve carrots and asparagus as side dishes.

Serves 4.

Martin Scott, Executive Chef, CEC

Born in Glasgow, Scotland, Chef Martin joined the Royal Caribbean International family in 1998. His experience is varied and includes companies such as the National Saudi Arabia Airline and various 5-star hotels. When not working, Chef Martin likes spending time with his wife and 3 children. He also very much enjoys reading and going to the movies.

CHICKEN

1¹/2 pounds (700 g) chicken legs, skinned and boned

1¹/2 pounds (700 g) chicken breast, skinned, boned and cut into 2-inch (5 cm) pieces

¹/4 cup (60 ml) vegetable oil

2 cloves garlic, chopped

1 tablespoon (15 g) peeled and chopped fresh ginger

2 tablespoons (30 ml) extra virgin olive oil

Salt and freshly ground black pepper

ORANGE CHILI SAUCE

¹/2 cup (120 ml) freshly squeezed orange juice

¹/4 cup (60 ml) frozen orange juice concentrate, thawed

1 cup (250 ml) sweet chili sauce

Zest of 1 orange, minced

Salt

JASMINE RICE

1¹/2 cups (400 g) jasmine rice

1¹/2 cups (400 ml) cold water

¹/2 pound (250 g) snow peas

2 tablespoons (30 g) unsalted butter

GARNISH

1 large green bell pepper, julienned and placed in ice water

1 large red bell pepper, julienned and placed in ice water

1 large carrot, julienned and placed in ice water

1 large leek, julienned and placed in ice water, white parts only

¹/3 cup (90 g) alfalfa sprouts

ORANGE CHILI CHICKEN

WINE PAIRING – ❦ – JOHANNISBERG RIESLING, CHATEAU ST. MICHELLE, COLUMBIA VALLEY, WASHINGTON

In a large bowl mix chicken with vegetable oil, garlic, ginger, salt and pepper. Cover and refrigerate for at least one hour.

Prepare orange chili sauce by mixing all ingredients in a medium saucepan. Bring mixture to a boil, then reduce heat and simmer for 10 minutes, stirring occasionally. Set aside.

In a large sauté pan over medium-high heat, warm olive oil and sauté chicken pieces for 5 minutes, until browned on all sides. Add orange chili sauce and cook over medium high heat for 10 to 15 minutes until chicken is cooked throughout and nicely glazed.

Rinse rice with cold water 3 to 4 times or until water runs clear. Drain one last time.

Place rice in a pot; add water, let stand for 30 minutes and bring to a boil. The liquid should be 1 inch (2.5 cm) above the rice. Cook, covered, for 15 minutes. Remove rice from heat and keep covered on the side of stove for 20 minutes.

Blanch snow peas, drain them and then sauté them in butter for 2 minutes. Season with salt and pepper.

Drain julienned vegetables and mix together with alfalfa sprouts just before serving.

Arrange chicken on a bed of rice and snow peas on a warmed dish, coat with orange chili sauce and top with julienned vegetables.

Serves 8.

CULINARY NOTES:

There are more than 40,000 different varieties of rice. It is classified according to its size: long-grain, medium-grain and short-grain. Rices are also labeled according to variety: Arborio, Aromatic, Basmati, Glutinous, Jasmine and Wehani. Each has its own characteristics and imparts its own special flavor and texture to the finished dish. Cooking techniques vary according to the type of rice. Some require soaking overnight while others need to be sautéed before boiling.

CHIMICHURRI SAUCE

Juice of 1 lemon
1/3 cup (90 g) minced fresh parsley
1 clove garlic, minced
2 shallots, small diced
2 tablespoons (30 g) minced fresh basil
2 tablespoons (30 g) minced fresh mint
1 teaspoon (5 g) minced hot pepper
1/2 tablespoon (7.5 ml) Worcestershire sauce
1 tablespoon (15 ml) soy sauce
1/4 red bell pepper, small diced
1/4 green bell pepper, small diced
1/2 cup (120 ml) extra virgin olive oil
Salt and freshly ground black pepper

GARLIC CONFIT

1 head of garlic, peeled and shaved
1/3 cup (90 ml) extra virgin olive oil

BALSAMIC VINAIGRETTE

1/4 cup (60 ml) balsamic vinegar
1/2 cup (120 ml) extra virgin olive oil
Salt and freshly ground black pepper

PORTABELLA

3 large portabella mushrooms, stalks and gills removed
2 tablespoons (30 ml) extra virgin olive oil
1/4 bunch parsley, finely chopped
1/4 bunch basil, finely chopped
Salt and freshly ground black pepper

SAUTÉED SPINACH

1 tablespoon (15 ml) extra virgin olive oil
1/2 onion, finely chopped
1/2 pound fresh spinach, stems off
Salt and freshly ground black pepper

STEAKS

6 (5-ounce) (150 g) New York strip steaks
Salt and freshly ground black pepper

FOCACCIA

6 individual rosemary focaccia, grilled (purchased)

GARNISH

1 cup (250 g) mesclun mix

OPEN FACE STEAK SANDWICH

WINE PAIRING – – WHITE ZINFANDEL, BERINGER, CALIFORNIA

Preheat oven to 325°F or 165°C.

For chimichurri sauce, combine all ingredients in a stainless steel bowl and slowly whisk in oil. Cover and refrigerate for 24 hours.

In a small saucepan over low heat, simmer garlic in olive oil for 20 minutes or until garlic reaches a light golden color.

To make vinaigrette, place vinegar in a small non-reactive bowl and slowly whisk in olive oil. Season with salt and black pepper to taste.

Cut portabella mushrooms into 5 slices at an angle. Brush with garlic confit and season with salt and pepper.

To Grill Mushrooms:

Outdoor grill: Heat to medium high. Place mushroom slices on the grill. Cook each slice for 2 to 3 minutes, turning only once. Remove from the grill and set on a tray.

Indoor grill: Lightly oil a grill pan. Set temperature to medium/high heat. Place mushroom slices on the grill. Cook each slice for 2 to 3 minutes, turning only once. Remove and set on a tray.

Top grilled mushroom slices with garlic confit and chopped herbs. Keep warm in the oven.

For spinach, in a saucepan over medium heat, warm oil and sauté onions for 4 minutes or until translucent. Add spinach and seasoning and sauté for 2 minutes. Drain excess water.

For steaks, preheat broiler for 5 minutes over high heat. Broil steaks to the desired degree of doneness, about 5 minutes for rare and 7 minutes for medium. Season with salt and pepper. Transfer to a warmed platter, tent loosely with aluminum foil and let stand for 10 minutes. Cut each steak in half at an angle.

Place focaccia on warmed plates, top with spinach, mushrooms, steaks and 2 spoonfuls of chimichurri sauce. Garnish with mesclun mix and drizzle with balsamic vinaigrette.

Serves 6.

IRISH CABBAGE

2 small Savoy cabbage, finely shredded
2 carrots, peeled and finely sliced

1 tablespoon (15 ml) extra virgin olive oil
1 tablespoon (15 g) butter
8 slices of bacon, diced
4 shallots, finely sliced
1/4 cup (60 ml) chicken stock (page 158)
Salt and freshly ground black pepper

LAMB

6 (7-ounce) (200 g) lamb tenderloin
2 tablespoons (30 ml) extra virgin olive oil
2 tablespoons (30 ml) sherry vinegar
1/2 bottle Cabernet wine
1 cup (250 ml) chicken stock (page 158)
Salt and freshly ground black pepper

MASHED POTATOES

2 pounds (1 kg) Idaho potatoes,
peeled, quartered
3/4 cup (175 ml) heavy cream
2 tablespoons (30 g) unsalted butter
Nutmeg
Salt and freshly ground black pepper

GARNISH

1/4 bunch parsley, finely chopped

IRISH LAMB AND CABBAGE

Andrew Cartwright, Executive Chef, CEC

Born in Bradford, England, Chef Andrew joined Royal Caribbean International in 2004. He is a graduate from the Thomas Danby Culinary School in Leeds, England and is a Certified Executive Chef from the American Culinary Federation. He trained in the best restaurants in Europe before finally giving in to his second passion and deciding to travel the world onboard first class vessels as Executive Chef, thus combining his love of food and travel. When not cooking, he enjoys playing golf, racing his Yamaha One motorcycle and spending time with his family and friends. Andrew also enjoys working in small restaurants around his hometown to keep up with current food trends.

Blanch cabbage in boiling salted water for 2 minutes. Remove from boiling water, cool in ice, drain and set aside. Return salted water to a boil, blanch carrots for 2 minutes. Cool in ice, drain and set aside.

In a pan, over medium heat, warm oil and butter and sauté bacon and shallots for 3 minutes. Add cabbage, carrots and stock and cook for 10 minutes or until vegetables are cooked through. Season with salt and pepper.

Season lamb with salt and pepper. In a sauté pan over high heat, warm oil and sear lamb on both sides. Reduce heat to medium and cook for 6 to 8 minutes, turning occasionally. Remove lamb and set aside. Deglaze sauté pan with sherry vinegar, add wine and reduce by half.

Add chicken stock and reduce until sauce is thick enough to coat the back of a spoon. Pass through a fine sieve or cheesecloth. Adjust seasoning with salt and pepper.

Place lamb back in sauce, cover and set aside.

Just before serving, slice loins diagonally into 4 slices each.

For mashed potatoes, place potatoes into cold, salted water, bring to a boil and cook until potatoes are easily pierced with the tip of a knife, about 15 minutes. Drain and press potatoes through a potato ricer into a heated bowl. Stir in cream, butter and nutmeg. Adjust seasoning with salt and pepper.

Place vegetables in the center of warm plates. Top with lamb. Ladle with sauce.

Serve mashed potatoes garnished with chopped parsley in a side dish.

Serves 6.

LAMB

1 (5 pounds) (2.3 kg) semi-boneless leg of lamb,
fat trimmed to 1/4 inch thick and tied
1 yellow onion, thickly sliced
1 carrot, chopped
2 tablespoons (30 ml) extra virgin olive oil
Salt and freshly ground black pepper

PASTE

5 cloves garlic, finely chopped
1/2 cup (115 g) breadcrumbs
1/2 tablespoon (7.5 ml) honey
1/2 tablespoon (7.5 g) mustard
1/4 teaspoon (1 g) sea salt
1/2 teaspoon (2.5 g) leave chopped rosemary

VEGETABLES

3 pounds new baby potatoes
cut into 1-inch or 2.5 cm pieces
3 large sweet potatoes
cut into 1-inch or 2.5 cm pieces
2 medium yellow onions, peeled and quartered
1 garlic head, peeled
1/4 cup (60 ml) extra virgin olive oil
Salt and freshly ground black pepper

NEW ZEALAND LEG OF LAMB

Preheat oven to 350°F or 175°C.

Place leg of lamb in a roasting pan atop onion and carrots, drizzle with oil and season with salt and pepper.

Roast lamb in middle of oven for 30 minutes.

In a small stainless steel or glass bowl, combine all ingredients for the paste and mix well.

Place vegetables in a large roasting pan. Drizzle with olive oil and season with salt and pepper. Hand mix thoroughly.

Remove semi-cooked lamb from the oven and place atop vegetables. Brush lamb with paste and return to the oven for 40 minutes or until an instant-read thermometer inserted 2 inches into the thickest part of meat (do not touch bone) registers 130°F or 55°C for medium.

Transfer to a cutting board, cover loosely and let stand 15 minutes.

Slice and arrange on plates surrounded by vegetables.

Serves 6.

David Reihana, Executive Chef, CEC

A native of Christchurch, New Zealand, Chef David has worked in several 5-star hotels such as the Balmoral in Scotland and the Ritz Carlton in Australia before joining the Royal Caribbean International family 5 years ago. His approach to food is simple. His love of cooking drives him to create dishes high in flavor and subtle in taste. Chef David's hobbies are fishing, rugby and riding his Harley Davidson® on the weekends around the lakes of the beautiful South Island.

VEAL SCALOPPINE

12 veal scaloppine, 1 1/2 to 2 inches (5 cm) thick
12 sage leaves
12 prosciutto slices, thin
Salt and freshly ground black pepper
1/2 cup (120 g) flour
6 tablespoons (85 ml) clarified unsalted butter
1/4 cup (60 ml) Marsala
1 cup (250 ml) dry white wine
2 cups (500 ml) veal demi-glace (page 159)
1 tablespoon (15 g) unsalted butter

RISOTTO

1/3 cup (90 g) dried porcini mushrooms
7-8 cups (1.5 to 2 L) chicken or vegetable stock (page 158)
1/4 cup (60 ml) extra virgin olive oil
2 shallots, finely chopped
1 clove garlic, chopped
3 cups (750 g) Arborio rice
1/2 cup (120 ml) dry white wine
2 tablespoons (30 g) unsalted butter
1/4 cup (60 g) Parmesan cheese, freshly grated
Salt and freshly ground white pepper

1 tablespoon (15 ml) extra virgin olive oil
1/3 cup (100 g) fresh crimini mushrooms, thickly sliced

12 baby zucchini, halved lengthways
1 tablespoon (15 ml) extra virgin olive oil
Salt and freshly ground black pepper

GARNISH

Fresh sage leaves

SALTIMBOCCA ALLA ROMANA
Veal Saltimbocca Romana

WINE PAIRING — CHIANTI CLASSICO RISERVA, CASTELLO DE GABBIANO, TUSCANY, ITALY

Flatten the veal fairly thin with the flat side of a mallet. Season with salt and black pepper, then place a fresh sage leaf and prosciutto on top of each scaloppine. To keep the prosciutto in place during cooking, place the ready meat between layers of plastic wrap and pound gently with the flat side of the mallet.

Dredge meat in flour. Shake off any excess.

Heat clarified unsalted butter in a large skillet and sauté veal for 1 minute on each side, starting with ham side down. Remove from pan and keep warm.

Using the same pan, add Marsala, then the wine and reduce slightly. Add veal demi-glace and reduce by half. Remove from heat. Strain into a small saucepan and whisk in butter. Keep warm.

For risotto, place dried mushrooms in warm water for 15 minutes.

In a saucepan over medium heat, bring stock to a simmer and maintain over low heat.

In a large saucepan, heat olive oil over medium heat. Add shallots and garlic and sauté until translucent, about 4 minutes Add dried mushrooms and rice and stir until each grain is well coated with oil, about 3 minutes. Add wine and stir until it is completely absorbed. Add stock to rice a ladleful at a time, stirring frequently after each addition until absorbed. Make sure the rice never gets dry. Season with salt and white pepper.

When rice is tender, about 20 minutes, add butter and grated cheese. Set aside.

Over medium heat, in a small saucepan, warm olive oil and sauté crimini mushrooms for 3 minutes.

Over low heat add a little of remaining stock to rice and sautéed mushrooms and warm up, about 1 minute.

Season zucchini and rub with olive oil. Heat a grilling pan over medium heat and grill for five minutes, turning once.

Serve risotto on a warmed plate, topped with veal. Garnish with grilled zucchini and a spoonful of Marsala reduction.

Serves 6.

CULINARY NOTES:

Butter is clarified to eliminate milk solids. To clarify, place butter in a small container and slowly heat until the proteins in the unsalted butter coagulate and rise to the surface while the solids sink to the bottom. Skim off the coagulated proteins from the top and carefully ladle out the now clarified butter, leaving the milk solids at the bottom.

Patrick McCabe, Executive Chef, CEC

Chef Patrick started his culinary career in his mother's kitchen, learning the basics from this accomplished cook. He completed his apprenticeship at Sheeky's Restaurant, a renowned seafood restaurant in London's Theater district. There he refined his skills by participating in an exchange program with the Badrutt's Palace Hotel of St. Moritz. Patrick joined Royal Caribbean International in 2002 after working for numerous deluxe hotels in Europe such as the Park Lane Hotel in Piccadilly. From there he emigrated to Australia, experimenting with "bush tucker" cuisine while working at the Victorian Art Center and the Grand Chancellor Hotel in Melbourne. When not onboard he enjoys bicycling and spending time with his family.

VEAL CHOPS

Juice of 2 lemons
1/4 cup (60 ml) extra virgin olive oil
Salt and freshly ground black pepper
6 (7-ounce or 200 g) veal chops

GALETTES

1/2 teaspoon (2 ml) vegetable oil
2 ounces (60 g) bacon, diced
1/2 onion, finely chopped
1 clove garlic, crushed
1/3 cup (100 g) cream cheese

1 tablespoon (15 ml) vegetable oil

4 large russet potatoes, peeled and grated (do not rinse)
3 tablespoons (45 g) clarified butter
Salt and freshly ground white pepper

MERLOT GLAZE

1 tablespoon (15 ml) vegetable oil
1 large carrot, finely chopped
2 onions, finely chopped
1 leek, cleaned and finely chopped
1/4 cup (60 g) finely chopped celery
1/2 cup (120 ml) Merlot wine
2 cups (450 ml) chicken stock (page 158)
2 tablespoons (30 g) butter
Salt and freshly ground black pepper

VEGETABLES

3 large carrots, cut in ribbons using a vegetable peeler
3 zucchinis, cut in ribbons using a vegetable peeler
1 tablespoon (15 g) butter
Salt and freshly ground white pepper

GARNISH

6 basil leaves, fried

GRILLED VEAL CHOPS
On Crispy Potato Galette with Merlot Glaze

Preheat oven to 350°F or 180°C.

For veal chops, in a stainless steel bowl, mix lemon juice, olive oil, salt and pepper. Coat veal chops with marinade. Cover and refrigerate for 1 hour.

For galettes, in a sauté pan over medium heat, warm oil and sauté bacon for 2 minutes or until crispy; add onion and garlic and cook for 3 minutes or until translucent; add cream cheese and mix well. Set aside.

In a large stainless steel bowl, mix potatoes with butter and seasoning.

Divide 1/2 of potato mixture into 6 lightly oiled small molds and press firmly. Fill in with cream cheese mixture and top with remaining potatoes. Press firmly and bake for 35 minutes.

For glaze, in a saucepan over medium heat, warm oil and sauté vegetables for 3 minutes. Deglaze with wine and reduce by half. Add chicken stock, bring to a boil and simmer for 30 minutes, skimming regularly

or until sauce coats the back of a wooden spoon. Remove from heat, strain into a small saucepan, rectify seasoning with salt and pepper and whisk in butter a little at a time. Keep warm.

Heat a grilling pan over high heat. Sear each side of chops for approximately 3 minutes. Arrange chops on a sheet pan and bake for about 20 minutes for medium cooked chops.

Blanch carrots in boiling salted water for 2 minutes. Drain and set aside.

Blanch zucchini in boiling salted water for 2 minutes. Drain and set aside.

In a small sauté pan over medium heat, melt butter and sauté vegetables for 2 minutes. Season with salt and pepper. Keep warm.

Arrange galette in the center of a warmed plate. Top with veal chop and garnish with vegetable ribbons and a spoonful of Merlot reduction. Finish with fried basil leaves.

Serves 6.

MARINADE

2-ounces (56 g) fresh ginger, peeled and grated

5 cloves garlic, peeled and grated

1 teaspoon (5 g) salt

1 tablespoon (15 g) turmeric powder

2 medium size chickens, skinned
and cut into 8 to 10 pieces or

12 chicken thighs, skinned and
3 chicken breasts, skinned and halved

PASTE

2-ounces (56 g) poppy seeds
soaked in hot water for 30 minutes

2-ounces (56 g) cashew nuts

SAUCE

¼ cup (60 g) Ghee or unsalted butter

2 yellow onions, peeled and sliced

1 tablespoon ground cinnamon

5 cloves

6 green cardamom pods

2 tablespoons ground coriander

½ teaspoon ground turmeric

2 bay leaves

2 cups (465 g) curd (natural milk yogurt)

1½ tablespoons (27 g) chili powder

¼ cup (120 ml) heavy cream

4-ounces (113 g) slivered almonds

Salt

RICE

1 tablespoon (15 g) vegetable oil

1 small yellow onion, thinly sliced

1 teaspoon (5 g) cumin seeds

6 black peppercorns

2 cloves

2 cardamom pods

1 bay leaf

½ cinnamon stick

1 teaspoon (5 g) salt

1 cup (235 g) Basmati rice, soaked in
cold water for 20 minutes, then drained

2 cups (475 ml) water

2 tablespoons (30 g) heavy cream

½ cup (115 g) frozen peas

2 tablespoons (30 g) chopped almonds

2 tablespoons (30 g) chopped cashew nuts

3 tablespoons (45 g) raisins

GARNISH

¼ bunch cilantro

MURG BADAMI
Chicken in Almond Cream

In a small stainless steel or glass bowl, mix ginger, garlic, salt and turmeric. Place chicken pieces into a deep dish and rub with marinade. Cover with plastic wrap and refrigerate for 30 minutes.

For paste, drain poppy seeds and transfer into a food processor. Add cashew nuts and blend to a fine paste.

In a large sauté pan over medium heat, melt butter (Ghee) and sauté onions for 8 to 10 minutes or until onions are well browned. Transfer onions to a plate, squeezing out excess fat. Return pan to heat and add cinnamon, cloves, cardamom pods, coriander, turmeric and bay leaves. Cook for 1 minute. Increase heat to medium high and sauté marinated chicken for 7 to 8 minutes or until it changes color, stirring continuously. Add yogurt, bring to a simmer, cover and cook for 15 minutes.

Reserve ¼ of the sautéed onions and place the remaining onto the chicken. Add nut paste, chili, ½ of the slivered almonds and heavy cream. Simmer for 10 minutes or until chicken is fully cooked. Season with salt.

Meanwhile, in a heavy stockpot over medium heat, warm oil and sauté onion for 5 minutes or until golden-brown. Incorporate spices and sauté for 3 minutes. Add rice and stir for 2 minutes. Add water and cream and bring to a boil. Reduce heat and simmer, covered, for 20 minutes or until rice is cooked and liquid is almost absorbed. Fold in peas and cook for 5 minutes or until peas are warmed through.

At the last minute, remove bay leaf and cinnamon and mix in nuts and raisins.

Spoon chicken in warmed bowls and garnish with cilantro and slivered almonds.

Serve rice in a separate bowl as a side dish topped with remaining sautéed onions.

Serves 6.

Anil George, Executive Chef, CEC

Chef Anil comes to us all the way from Poona City, located about 160 kms from Mumbai, India. After completing his degree in Hotel Management in Dubai, where he specialized in Nutrition and Catering Technology, he worked on land for a few years before starting his career at sea. Chef Anil joined Royal Caribbean in 1991 and has worked his way through the ranks and throughout the entire fleet. When not sailing he spends his time with his family. He also very much enjoys traveling the world to discover new cuisines and visit friends.

SHALLOT CONFIT

3 shallots, peeled and shaved
2 cloves garlic, peeled and shaved
1/3 cup (90 ml) extra virgin olive oil

MASHED POTATOES

2 pounds (1 kg) Yukon Gold potatoes, peeled, quartered
1/2 cup (120 ml) heavy cream
2 tablespoons (30 g) unsalted butter
Salt and freshly ground white pepper

TOMATO CONFIT

1/4 cup (60 g) sugar
6 cracked black peppercorns
2 bay leaves
1 cup (240 ml) Madeira

10-ounces (295 g) grape tomatoes, halved
1/4 bunch fresh basil, chiffonade
1 teaspoon (5 g) oregano
1 teaspoon (5 g) thyme
1 teaspoon (5 g) rosemary

MUSHROOMS

8 medium size portabella mushrooms, stem and gills removed
Salt and freshly ground black pepper

GORGONZOLA BUTTER

1/2 cup (115 g) butter, softened
3-ounces (85 g) Gorgonzola cheese, coarsely cut
Freshly ground white pepper

STEAKS

8 (8-ounce) (200 g) New York strip steaks
1 tablespoon (15 ml) extra virgin olive oil
Salt and freshly ground black pepper

GARNISH

Fresh rosemary sprigs

GRILLED NY STRIP STEAK

WINE PAIRING – ⍾ – SYRAH, L'ECOLE NO. 41, "SEVEN HILLS VINEYARD," WALLA WALLA, WASHINGTON

Preheat oven to 400°F or 205°C.

For shallot confit, in a small saucepan over medium heat, simmer shallots and garlic in olive oil for 20 minutes. Do not brown. Allow to cool. Cover and reserve.

For mashed potatoes, place potatoes into salted cold water, bring to a boil and cook until potatoes are easily pierced with the tip of a knife, about 15 minutes. Drain and press potatoes through a potato ricer into a heated bowl. Stir in cream and butter. Adjust seasoning with salt and pepper. Set aside and keep warm.

To make the tomato confit, in a small saucepan over medium heat, combine sugar, cracked pepper, bay leaves and Madeira and simmer until syrupy.

Meanwhile, place half of the shallot confit into a sauté pan over medium heat, add tomatoes and herbs and cook for 5 minutes. Fold in Madeira reduction a little at a time until reaching the desired sweetness.

Place mushrooms on a greased sheet pan. Brush heavily with remaining shallot confit, season with salt and pepper and bake for 5 minutes. Remove from heat and fill with tomato mixture. Return to oven for another 5 minutes.

In a small glass or stainless steel bowl, gently mix butter and gorgonzola. Season with pepper. Keep semi cold.

For steaks, preheat broiler for 5 minutes over high heat. Broil seasoned steaks to the desired degree of doneness, about 5 minutes for rare and 7 minutes for medium. Transfer to a warmed platter, tent loosely with aluminum foil and let stand for 5 minutes.

On warmed entrée plates, place steak at an angle over mashed potatoes and top with a small spoonful of gorgonzola butter. Delicately transfer a confit filled portabella mushroom to each plate and garnish with rosemary sprig.

Serves 8.

CULINARY NOTES:

Chiffonade (French word meaning made from rags) is a technique for cutting herbs or leafy vegetables into long, thin strips. The best way to chiffonade basil or other broad leaf herbs (mint, sage, etc) is to pick the leaves and stack them, one on top of the other. Using a sharp Chef's knife at a 45 degree angle to the spine of the leaf - chop into thin ribbons. Some Chefs roll the stack of leaves into a cigar shape before cutting. This is a quick and easy way to "chiff" a large quantity of herbs. The problem is you will inevitably end up with at least one ribbon that is all spine.

WASABI SAUCE

2 to 3 teaspoons (10 g) wasabi powder
1 cup (250 ml) Chardonnay wine
1 cup (250 ml) heavy cream
Juice of 1/2 lemon
1/2 teaspoon (2 g) salt
2 tablespoons (30 g) unsalted butter,
room temperature

FILETS

4 (6 to 7-ounce) (170 to 200 g) filet
mignon steaks
2 tablespoons (30 ml) extra virgin olive oil
Salt and freshly ground black pepper

RICE BALLS

2 cups (500 g) sushi rice
2 cups (500 ml) cold water
1/2 teaspoon (2 g) Mirin wine
1/2 teaspoon (2 g) sake
1 teaspoon (5 g) icing sugar

1/4 cup (60 g) all purpose flour
1/4 cup (60 g) corn starch
3 egg yolks
1 cup (250 ml) cold water
Salt
1 cup (250 ml) vegetable oil for frying

STIR-FRIED VEGETABLES

1 1/2 tablespoons (25 ml) vegetable oil
1/2 tablespoon (10 ml) sesame oil
2 green onions cut lengthwise
1 clove garlic, crushed
1/4 fresh red chili, seeded and sliced
1/2 cup (120 g) snow peas, blanched
1/2 cup (120 g) cauliflower florettes, blanched
1/2 cup (120 g) broccoli florettes, blanched
1/4 cup (60 g) carrots, cut diagonally and
blanched
1/2 red bell pepper, cut in strips
2 tablespoons (30 ml) soy sauce
1 tablespoon (15 ml) fish sauce
1 tablespoon (15 ml) oyster sauce
3 tablespoons (45 ml) vegetable stock (page 158)

*Wim Van Der Pas, Culinary Trainer
for the Royal Culinary Academy at Sea*

Chef Wim joined Royal Caribbean International in 2003. Wim was born in Vught, Netherlands, but has lived in New Zealand for the past 17 years with his wife, Christine and their 3 children, Cameron, Zeranya and Rinaldo. His culinary career began at the age of 12, working after school in restaurants as a pot washer. After attending culinary school in the Netherlands, he worked throughout Europe and New Zealand in some of those countries' most renowned establishments. When not onboard, Wim enjoys playing soccer with his children or watching a good rugby game.

FILET MIGNON GOES EAST

Prepare wasabi by mixing the powder with 2 to 3 teaspoons (10 to 15 ml) of water until it reaches a paste consistency.

To make sauce, bring wine to a boil in a medium size saucepan and simmer for about 10 minutes until wine has reduced by half. Stir in cream and simmer for 5 minutes, until mixture is thick enough to coat the back of a spoon. Add lemon juice, salt and wasabi paste. Remove from heat and whisk in butter a little at a time. Adjust seasoning with salt if necessary. Keep warm.

Rinse rice with cold water 3 to 4 times or until water runs clear. Drain one last time.

Place rice in a pot; add water, let stand for 30 minutes and bring to a boil. The liquid should be 1 inch (2.5 cm) above the rice. Cook, covered, for 15 minutes. Remove rice from heat and keep covered on the side of stove for 20 minutes. In a small saucepan combine wine, sake and icing sugar. Heat mixture until sugar is dissolved. Place rice into a sushi barrel or large bowl, pour vinegar mixture evenly over rice, mix and let cool.

To make batter, sift flour and corn starch into a large bowl, whisk in egg yolks and water. Season with salt and mix well.

Once rice has cooled, form it into 2-inch (5 cm) balls. Dip balls in the batter and fry until golden brown.

For the stir fry, heat wok or frying pan over medium heat, warm oils and add green onion, garlic and chili. Stir fry for 1 minute; add vegetables and stir fry for 2 minutes over high heat. Stir in sauces and stock. Cook for 5 minutes, until the vegetables are tender but still with a little crunch.

Rub steaks with the oil and season with salt and pepper.

Heat grill and sear filets on both sides. Reduce heat and cook until desired doneness.

Arrange stir-fried vegetables in the center of warmed plates. Place meat on top. Garnish with tempura rice balls. Spoon some wasabi sauce over meat and serve immediately.

Serves 4.

MARINADE

3 cloves garlic, peeled and shaved
1 tablespoon (15 g) thyme
1/4 cup (60 ml) extra virgin olive oil
1/4 cup (60 ml) white wine
Salt and freshly ground black pepper
4 (5-ounce) (150 g) veal tenderloin medallions
1/4 cup (60 g) all-purpose flour
1 tablespoon (15 ml) vegetable oil
2 (6-ounce) (170 g) lobster tails

MASHED POTATOES

2 pounds (1 kg) Idaho potatoes
4 ounces (120 g) mascarpone cheese
1/4 cup (60 ml) milk
Salt and freshly ground white pepper

BEURRE BLANC

2 shallots, minced
6 black peppercorns, crushed
1/3 cup (90 ml) dry white wine
Juice of 1 lemon
3 tablespoons (45 ml) cider vinegar
1/2 cup (120 ml) heavy cream
1 pound (450 g) unsalted butter,
    room temperature
1/2 bunch basil, finely chopped
Salt and freshly ground black pepper

BROWN SAUCE

2 shallots, minced
1/4 cup (60 ml) brandy
3/4 cup (175 ml) brown sauce (page 159)

GARNISH

12 asparagus spears, trimmed and peeled

ROYAL VEAL, BASIL BEURRE BLANC AND MASCARPONE MASHED POTATOES

In a stainless steel bowl, mix all ingredients for marinade. Remove lobster meat from shells. Place two skewers in lobster meat to keep them straight. Marinate tails for 2 hours, covered and refrigerated.

Place potatoes into salted cold water, bring to a boil and cook until potatoes are easily pierced with the tip of a knife, about 15 minutes. Drain and press potatoes through a potato ricer into a heated bowl. Add mascarpone cheese and milk. Adjust seasoning and keep warm.

For the beurre blanc, combine shallots, peppercorns, wine, lemon juice and vinegar in a saucepan. Simmer for 7 minutes until the sauce liquids are reduced by two-thirds. Add cream and simmer for 10 minutes. Do not boil. Remove from heat and whisk in the butter a little at a time. Strain through a sieve. Adjust seasoning with salt and pepper, stir in basil and keep warm.

Preheat oven to 400°F or 200°C.

Pat dry veal medallions, season with salt and pepper and dredge in flour. Shake off any excess. In a sauté pan over high heat, warm oil and pan-sear both sides for 5 minutes or until golden brown. Transfer medallions to a baking sheet. For brown sauce, pour off any excess oil from the saucepan, add shallots and sauté for 3 minutes, until translucent and deglaze with brandy. Add brown sauce and simmer until sauce has reduced by half. Strain and keep warm.

In a sauté pan over medium-high heat, sear lobster tails for 5 minutes on each side. Remove from heat, remove skewers and cut into 1 inch (2.5 cm) thick medallions.

Blanch asparagus in boiling, salted water for 3 minutes.

To serve, transfer potatoes to a piping bag and pipe into the center of warm plates, top with veal, then lobster medallions. Spoon some beurre blanc over the lobsters and some brown sauce around the plate. Garnish with asparagus.

Serves 4.

Marco Marrama,
Senior Executive Chef, CEC

Chef Marco joined Royal Caribbean International in 2003 as an Executive Sous Chef onboard Voyager of the Seas. Marco was born and raised in Rome, Italy. He attended culinary school in Rome and obtained a diploma in classic French Cuisine, as well as a culinary diploma from the Cordon Bleu school in Rome. He has worked in fine dining restaurants in Europe, Australia and at the Royal Palace in Skirat, Morocco. When not cooking, Marco enjoys painting, playing tennis and taking care of his bonsai.

Vegetarian

ROASTED PEPPERS
2 red bell peppers
2 tablespoons (30 ml) extra virgin olive oil

VEGETABLES
2 tablespoons (30 ml) extra virgin olive oil
2 zucchini, sliced
1 medium eggplant, sliced
12 thin asparagus
Salt and freshly ground black pepper

MARINADE
3 tablespoons (45 ml) extra virgin olive oil
2 cloves garlic, peeled and chopped
¼ bunch basil, finely chopped

CORN PANCAKES
2½ cups (580 g) corn kernels, defrosted
1 small red onion, chopped
2 eggs
¼ bunch cilantro, chopped
1 cup (235 g) all-purpose flour
1 teaspoon (15 g) baking powder
Salt and freshly ground black pepper

2 tablespoons (30 ml) vegetable oil

AVOCADO SALSA
2 ripe avocados, peeled, stone removed and diced
¼ bunch cilantro, finely chopped
2 plum tomatoes, diced
2 spring onions, finely chopped
2 tablespoons (30 ml) freshly squeezed lime juice
1 teaspoon (5 ml) Tabasco® hot sauce
Salt and freshly ground black pepper

GARNISH
½ cup (120 ml) sour cream
Cilantro sprigs

CORN PANCAKES

WINE PAIRING – ❦ – CONUNDRUM, CALIFORNIA

Preheat oven to 400°F or 200°C.

Place peppers in an ovenproof dish, drizzle with oil, season with salt and roast for 20 minutes or until peppers are brown and skin blisters.

Remove peppers from oven and place into a small bowl and cover with plastic wrap. A small, tightly closed bag will also do. This loosens the skins and eases peeling. Peel and cut lengthwise.

Reduce oven to 350°F or 175°C.

To grill vegetables, lightly oil a grill pan. Set temperature to medium/high heat. Brush vegetables with oil, season with salt and pepper and place on grilling pan. Cook each slice for approximately 4 minutes, turning only once. Place grilled vegetables on a sheet pan.

Meanwhile, in a small glass or stainless steel bowl, mix all ingredients for marinade. Pour marinade over grilled vegetables and set aside. Keep warm.

To make pancake batter, place ½ of corn and all remaining ingredients in a food processor and blend until smooth.

Transfer into a large glass or stainless steel bowl. Incorporate remaining corn and mix well.

Warm a griddle over medium heat and grease thoroughly.

Using a small ladle pour batter on griddle, forming 4-inch (10 cm) diameter pancakes and cook for 3 minutes on each side, turning once. Transfer pancakes on a sheet pan lined with paper towels. Keep warm in the oven, leaving the door open.

Prepare salsa by mixing all ingredients in a glass bowl.

To plate, place 2 corn pancakes in the center of warmed plates. Top with layers of roasted peppers and grilled vegetables. Finish with a spoonful of salsa, a dollop of sour cream, cilantro sprig and a drizzle of oil marinade.

Serves 6.

PIZZA DOUGH

2 1/2 teaspoons (15 g) active dry yeast
1 cup (250 ml) warm water
1 teaspoon (5 g) honey
1 tablespoon (15 ml) extra virgin olive oil
3 cups (700 g) all-purpose flour
1 teaspoon (5 g) salt

2 tablespoons (30 ml) extra virgin olive oil

FILLING

2 tablespoons (30 ml) extra virgin olive oil
2 cloves garlic, chopped
1 (28-ounce) (794 g) can whole peeled tomatoes
in juice, cut into strips
Salt and freshly ground black pepper
2 tablespoons (30 g) pesto
1/4 bunch fresh basil, julienned
2 cups (500 g) shredded Mozzarella cheese
1 egg

EGG WASH

1 egg, beaten

TOMATO SALAD

1 cup (235 g) grape tomatoes, halved
1 small red onion, small diced
1 clove garlic, chopped
1 tablespoon (15 g) chopped parsley
1 tablespoon (15 g) julienned basil
1/4 cup (60 ml) extra virgin olive oil
Salt and freshly ground black pepper

GARNISH

1/4 cup (60 g) shredded Mozzarella cheese
Julienned basil

TOMATO, BASIL AND MOZZARELLA CALZONE

WINE PAIRING – MARCHESI DI FRESCOBALDI, CHIANTI RUFINA, "CASTELLO DI NIPOZZANO," RISERVA, ITALY

Preheat oven to 500°F or 260°C.

For pizza dough, in a small bowl, dissolve yeast and water. Add honey and stir together. Let sit for 2 minutes or until water is cloudy. Add olive oil and mix well.

Place flour and salt in a food processor fitted with the blade attachment. Pulse a couple times then, with machine running, pour in yeast mixture and process until dough forms a ball. Transfer to lightly floured surface. Knead for 2 minutes adding flour as necessary until dough is smooth and elastic.

Place dough into a lightly oiled bowl. Cover with plastic wrap and let rise for 30 minutes in a warm spot.

Divide dough in 2 to 4 equal pieces. Hand roll into balls and place on a tray. Cover and let rest for 30 minutes.

Place ball on a lightly floured surface. While turning dough, press down on its center then use a rolling pin to get an even circle (8-inches or 20 cm).

Brush pizza with olive oil, avoiding rims. Transfer onto an oiled pizza pan.

Meanwhile, in a sauté pan over medium heat, warm oil and sweat off garlic for 3 minutes. Add tomatoes and cook until all liquid has absorbed. Season with salt and pepper and transfer to a perforated pan or colander to insure all liquid is removed. Reserve 1/4 cup (60 g) tomato mixture for the topping.

In a glass or stainless steel bowl, mix remaining tomato mixture with pesto, basil, mozzarella cheese and egg. Spread tomato-cheese filling on one half of the dough circle, leaving a border around it for closing. Close calzone by folding the unfilled side on top of the filled side. Crimp the edges with your fingers and ensure the dough is completely sealed.

Lightly brush with egg wash and bake for 20 minutes.

Meanwhile, in a glass or stainless steel bowl, mix all ingredients for the tomato salad. Season with salt and pepper and refrigerate.

Remove calzones from oven and brush the top with the reserved tomato sauce. Sprinkle with mozzarella cheese and put back in the oven for 5 minutes or until cheese has melted. Garnish with julienned basil.

Serve calzones hot with a side dish of tomato salad and your favorite Chianti.

Serves 4.

CULINARY NOTES:

Additional ingredients can be added to the filling to create a variety of different calzones: Pepperoni, Italian Sausage, peppers (fully-cooked), etc... It is recommended that you use no more than 3 ingredients total. Any more than that and the calzone will not cook through and the insides will be cold and mushy.

Craig Cornick, CEC, ACE
Culinary Trainer for the Royal Culinary
Academy at Sea

English Chef Trainer Craig joined Royal Caribbean International in 2004 after working in the UK for several years in various boutique hotels and restaurants. His love of traveling and sailing had him roam the 7 seas onboard several cruise liners where he specialized in the opening (and training) for new culinary outlets. Now living in West Java, Indonesia his priority, when not working, is to spend time with his wife and daughter Ira. His hobbies are golfing and playing soccer for the International expatriate Java football team.

SOUFFLÉS

2 cloves garlic, peeled and finely chopped
1 teaspoon vegetable oil

1/4 cup (60g) butter, plus a little extra
for greasing the soufflé cups
3 slices whole wheat bread,
lightly toasted then grated
3 1/2 tablespoons (57 g) all-purpose flour
1 teaspoon (5 g) Coleman's English mustard
Pinch of cayenne pepper
Pinch of nutmeg

2 cups (475 ml) milk, hot
6 eggs, separated
2 tablespoons (30 g) finely chopped chives
7-ounce (200 g) Wensleydale cheese cut in large
crumbles or good quality Cheddar cheese
Salt and freshly ground black pepper

ACCOMPANIMENTS

Celery sticks
4 Roma tomatoes cut in wedges
Classic English Branston Pickles, store bought

WENSLEYDALE CHEESE AND WHOLE WHEAT BREAD SOUFFLÉS

Preheat oven to 380°F or 195°C.

In a small baking sheet covered with parchment paper, gently toss garlic with oil and roast for 5 to 8 minutes or until golden brown. At the same time, place a baking tray on the lower level of your oven rack.

Lightly grease four soufflé cups with butter and dust whole wheat breadcrumbs onto the sides of the soufflé dishes.

In a saucepan over medium heat, melt butter and stir in flour, mustard, cayenne and nutmeg, reduce heat and cook gradually until the mixture bubbles. Mix in remaining breadcrumbs.

Reduce to slow heat and gently incorporate milk, a little at a time, stirring continuously. Cook for 2 minutes and let cool.

Once mixture is lukewarm, stir in egg yolks, chopped roasted garlic and chives. Slowly incorporate crumbled Wensleydale cheese and season with salt and pepper.

In a stainless steel or glass bowl, whisk the egg whites and a pinch of salt until it forms firm peaks and carefully fold into cheese mixture being careful not to knock the air out of the mixture and keeping it light and aerated.

Fill soufflé cups with cheese mixture and place cups onto the pre-heated baking tray in the oven. Bake for 10 to 12 minutes or until center of the soufflés are just wobbling.

Serve immediately with your favorite condiments.

Serves 4.

CULINARY NOTES:

Do not open the oven door until at least 10 minutes have passed to check on the soufflés.

MARINARA SAUCE

2 tablespoons (30 ml) extra virgin olive oil
1 onion, diced
1 clove garlic, chopped
6 ripe tomatoes, peeled, seeded and diced
1/2 teaspoon (2 g) chopped oregano
1/2 teaspoon (2 g) chopped basil
Salt and freshly ground black pepper

EGGPLANTS

2 to 3 medium eggplant, cut into
1/2-inch thick (1.2 cm) slices (approximately 18)
Salt and freshly ground black pepper
1 cup (250 g) all-purpose flour
2 eggs, beaten
1 cup (250 g) bread crumbs
1 cup (250 ml) vegetable oil

4 tomatoes, sliced 1/2-inch (1.2 cm) thick
(approximately 18 slices)
1 cup (250 g) shredded mozzarella

1/2 cup (120 ml) balsamic vinegar

1 broccoli spear, broken into florets
4 tablespoons (60 g) unsalted butter

GARNISH

Basil leaves

EGGPLANT MOZZARELLA TOWER

 WINE PAIRING – – MERLOT, ARBOLEDA, COLCHAQUA VALLEY, CHILE

Preheat oven to 350˚F or 180˚C.

For marinara, in a small saucepan over medium heat, warm oil and sauté onion for 4 minutes or until translucent. Add garlic and sauté, stirring continually. Do not brown. Add tomatoes and herbs and season with salt and pepper. Cover and simmer for 10 minutes. Set aside.

Season eggplant slices with salt and pepper and dredge in flour, shaking off the excess. Next dip each slice in egg, then in the bread crumbs. Set aside.

In a large skillet heat vegetable oil over high heat until very hot. Sauté eggplant one slice at a time until golden brown.

Place the cooked slices on a baking sheet, top each with a tomato slice and sprinkle with mozzarella. Bake for about 10 minutes, until golden brown and cheese is melted.

In a small saucepan, simmer vinegar until it's reduced by about two-thirds and reaches a syrup consistency. Set aside to cool.

Steam the broccoli florets for 3 minutes. In a small saucepan melt butter. Just before serving, dip the broccoli into butter to coat.

To serve, stack three eggplant/tomato slices on each plate. Garnish with a broccoli floret and basil. Spoon marinara around eggplant tower and drizzle with balsamic reduction.

Serves 6.

CULINARY NOTES:

Most eggplants produce a bitter-tasting alkaloid. A method for removing this unwanted flavor is to sprinkle the slices with salt and let them rest in a colander for an hour. Afterwards, rinse the slices under cold water, gently squeezing out the moisture. Pressing on the slices also collapses the eggplant's air pockets, reducing the absorption of oil during frying.

PIE CRUST

1 cup (250 g) all-purpose flour

½ teaspoon (2 g) salt

¼ cup (60 g) shortening, room temperature

3 tablespoons (45 ml) water

FILLING

1 tablespoon (15 ml) extra virgin olive oil

1 white onion, small diced

12 asparagus, peeled, blanched and cut into ½-inch (1.2 cm) dice

1 tablespoon (15 g) chopped parsley

1 tablespoon (15 g) chopped chives

½ tablespoon (10 g) chopped thyme

Salt and freshly ground black pepper

⅓ cup (100 g) shredded Gruyère cheese

8 ounces (230 g) Brie cheese, sliced

3 eggs

⅓ cup (100 ml) heavy cream

Salt and freshly ground black pepper

HERB EMULSION

1 cup (250 g) firmly packed fresh basil leaves (2 bunches)

½ bunch chives

½ bunch parsley, coarsely chopped

¾ cup (175 ml) extra virgin olive oil

Salt and freshly ground black pepper

SEMI-DRIED TOMATOES

3 Roma tomatoes, cut in half lengthwise

3 tablespoons (45 ml) garlic oil (purchased)

RED PEPPER REDUCTION

½ tablespoon (10 ml) extra virgin olive oil

3 red bell peppers

½ teaspoon (2 g) sugar

1 tablespoon (15 ml) Champagne vinegar

2 tablespoons (30 ml) water

BALSAMIC DRESSING

¼ cup (60 ml) extra virgin olive oil

¼ cup (60 ml) balsamic vinegar

1 teaspoon (5 g) fresh thyme leaves

Salt and freshly ground black pepper

GARNISH

8 ounce (250 g) arugula

ASPARAGUS AND BRIE TART

WINE PAIRING – ♟ – CHARDONNAY, CALITERRA, "TRIBUTO," CASABLANCA, CHILE

Preheat oven to 300°F or 150°C.

In a medium bowl, with a fork, lightly stir together flour and salt. With fork, cut shortening into flour until the mixture resembles coarse crumbs. Sprinkle cold water one teaspoon (5 ml) at a time, mixing lightly with fork after each addition, until pastry begins to hold together. With your hands, shape pastry into a ball. Refrigerate for 30 minutes.

On a lightly floured surface, roll pastry in ⅛-inch (0.3 cm) thick circle about 2-inches (5 cm) larger all around the pie molds.

Roll pastry circle gently onto rolling pin. Transfer to pie molds and unroll. With a sharp knife, trim edges, pinch to form a high edge and make a decorative edge by pressing it with a fork. Prick crusts with a fork to prevent puffing during baking. Refrigerate for ½ hour.

Blind bake pie crusts for 5 minutes, remove from oven and let cool.

While crust is baking, warm olive oil in a small saucepan over medium heat and sauté onions until translucent, about 4 minutes. Add asparagus, fresh herbs, salt and black pepper and sauté for 2 minutes. Do not brown.

Sprinkle tart shells with Gruyère cheese and evenly spread with asparagus mixture.

In a medium bowl, beat eggs lightly, add cream and seasonings. Beat until well mixed.

Pour mixture over cheese and asparagus. Top with sliced Brie. Bake for 20 minutes or until a skewer inserted in the tart comes out clean.

To prepare herb essence, blanch basil and chives in a pan of boiling water for 10 seconds. Drain and refresh in iced water. Pat dry with paper towels and transfer to a blender. Add parsley and oil and purée until smooth. Transfer to a small bowl. Season to taste with salt and pepper and strain using a fine sieve or cheesecloth. Cover and refrigerate until chilled.

Reduce oven to 200°F or 95°C.

Place tomatoes on a small sheet pan, drizzle with garlic oil and bake for 1 hour.

For red pepper reduction, if using a juice extractor, run peppers through your juice extractor. Transfer into a small saucepan, add sugar and vinegar and reduce for 15 minutes, over low heat, until reaching a glaze consistency.

Without a juice extractor, in a small saucepan over medium heat, warm olive oil and sauté sliced peppers for 10 minutes or until soft. Add sugar, vinegar and water and simmer until liquid reduces by half.

Transfer into a blender and purée until smooth. Strain with a cheesecloth and further reduce to a glaze consistency.

For balsamic dressing, in a mixing bowl, combine oil, vinegar, thyme, salt and pepper to taste. Mix well and transfer into a serving dish.

Serve tarts on warmed plates, crown with arugula and semi-dried tomatoes.

Drizzle plate with red pepper reduction and herb essence.

Serves 6.

WHITE SAUCE

2 tablespoons (30 g) butter
4 tablespoons (60 g) flour
1 cup (250 ml) milk
Salt and freshly ground white pepper

FILLING

1/2 onion, finely chopped
1 tablespoon (15 ml) extra virgin olive oil
1 cup (250 g) ricotta cheese
1/4 cup (60 g) grated Parmigiano-Reggiano cheese
1/2 pound (250 g) baby spinach, wilted
Salt and freshly ground black pepper

MARINARA SAUCE

2 tablespoons (30 ml) extra virgin olive oil
1 onion, diced
3 cloves garlic, chopped
6 ripe tomatoes, peeled, seeded and diced
1/2 teaspoon (2 g) chopped basil
Salt and freshly ground black pepper

MELANZANE

2 medium size eggplants, skinned and thinly sliced lengthwise
1/4 cup (60 g) flour
2 tablespoons (30 ml) extra virgin olive oil
1/4 cup (60 g) grated Parmigiano-Reggiano cheese

HERBED OIL

1/4 bunch basil
1/4 bunch parsley
1/4 bunch chives
1/2 cup (120 ml) extra virgin olive oil

GARNISH

12 shavings Parmigiano-Reggiano cheese
Fried basil leaves

MELANZANE RIPIENI DI RICOTTA E SPINACI ALLA PARMIGIANA

Eggplant roulades filled with ricotta and spinach, Parmesan style

WINE PAIRING – ZINFANDEL, RAVENSWOOD, "OLD VINE," SONOMA, CALIFORNIA

Preheat oven to 350°F or 180°C.

For white sauce, in a small stockpot, melt butter over medium heat; gradually add flour a spoonful at a time to create a roux. Cook over medium heat for 2 to 3 minutes. Do not brown. Slowly whisk in milk. Bring to a boil and stir consistently to avoid lumps. Season with salt and pepper.

In a small sauté pan over medium heat, sauté onions in oil for 3 minutes or until translucent. Add ricotta, season with salt and pepper and cook for 10 minutes. Combine with white sauce and Parmesan cheese.

In a sauté pan over medium heat, place spinach and pan-fry for 5 minutes. Season and squeeze all the water out of them. Add to ricotta mixture. Mix well and let cool.

For marinara, in a small saucepan over medium heat, warm oil and sauté onion and garlic for 4 minutes or until onions are translucent. Add tomatoes and basil and season with salt and pepper. Cover and simmer for 10 minutes. Set aside.

Toss eggplant slices in flour. Shake well to remove excess flour. In a frying pan over high heat, warm oil and fry eggplants 1 minute on each side. Set aside on a plate layered with absorbent paper.

On a lightly greased sheet pan, lay eggplant slices and fill with ricotta mixture. Roll and top with some marinara sauce, sprinkle with Parmesan cheese and bake for 10 minutes.

To prepare herbed oil, blanch herbs in a pan of boiling water for 10 seconds. Drain and refresh in iced water. Pat dry with paper and transfer to a blender. Add oil and purée until smooth. Using a fine sieve or cheesecloth, strain into a small bowl. Cover and set aside.

To serve, place a couple spoonfuls of marinara in the center of each warmed plate. Top with 2 eggplant rolls and the wilted spinach. Garnish with Parmesan shavings and fried basil. Finish with herbed oil drizzles.

Serves 6.

CULINARY NOTES:

You will want to purchase whole, solid Parmigiano-Reggiano cheese and grate or shave your own. The grated kind in the thin green tube is just not the same.

"Parmesan" is a common term for any cheese imitating true grana-style cheeses.

Grana-style cheese is a hard granular cheese that is cooked but not pressed. It is made from raw milk and aged for up to 12 months. Only milk produced from May 1 to November 11 is used in producing the true Parmigiano-Reggiano cheese.

VEGETABLE CURRY

2 tablespoons (30 ml) vegetable oil

2 tablespoons (30 g) peeled, minced fresh ginger

2 cloves garlic, minced

1 pound (450 g) Spanish onions cut
into 1/4-inch (0.6 cm) slices

1 teaspoon (5 g) curry powder

1 teaspoon (5 g) ground cumin

1 teaspoon (5 g) ground coriander

1 teaspoon (5 g) cayenne powder

1 teaspoon (5 g) ground turmeric

1 bay leaf

1/2 pound (250 g) carrots, peeled and
cut into 1/2-inch (1.2 cm) cubes

3/4 pound (350 g) potatoes, peeled and cut
into 1/2-inch (1.2 cm) cubes

1/4 pound (120 g) eggplant, cut
into 1/2-inch (1.2 cm) cubes

1 1/2 quarts (1.5 L) vegetable stock (page 158)

1/4 pound (120 g) cauliflower florets

1 pound (450 g) Roma tomatoes, cut
into 1/2-inch (1.2 cm) slices

1/4 pound (120 g) frozen okra, sliced
(keep frozen until ready to use)

1/4 bunch cilantro

1 pound (450 g) frozen peas

3 ounces (100 g) plain yogurt

Salt and freshly ground black pepper

JASMINE RICE

1 1/2 cups (400 g) Jasmine rice

1 1/2 cups (400 ml) cold water

6 (7-inch) (18 cm) flour tortillas, purchased

CUCUMBER RAITA

1 pound (450 g) cucumbers, peeled in alternate
strips, seeded and grated

1/2 cup (120 g) plain yogurt

1 tomato, peeled, seeded and cut
into 1/8-inch (0.3 cm) cubes

1/4 bunch mint, chopped

GARNISH

Pappadam, purchased

Fresh chervil

INDIAN VEGETABLE CURRY

WINE PAIRING – ♍ – VIOGNIER, BERINGER, NAPA VALLEY, CALIFORNIA

For curry, in a large sauté pan, heat oil over medium heat and add ginger, garlic, onions and all the spices. Sauté for about 5 minutes, until the onions are light blond and soft. Do not brown.

Add carrots, potatoes and eggplant and sauté for about 10 minutes.

Add vegetable stock, stir and bring to a boil. Add cauliflower, tomatoes, frozen okra and cilantro. Stir, cover and turn heat down to medium low. Simmer for 10 minutes and add frozen peas. Simmer for another 5 minutes or until all the vegetables are soft. Adjust seasoning with salt and pepper.

Just before serving swirl in yogurt.

Rinse rice with cold water 3 to 4 times or until water runs clear. Drain one last time.

Place rice in a pot; add water, let stand for 30 minutes and bring to a boil. The liquid should be 1 inch (2.5 cm) above the rice. Cook, covered, for 15 minutes. Remove rice from heat and keep covered on the side of stove for 20 minutes.

Preheat oven to 350°F or 180°C.

Place each tortilla in 4 inch (10 cm) ramekins and bake for 10 minutes or until lightly browned and set.

To prepare raita, mix cucumber, yogurt, tomato and mint.

On a warm plate, place tortilla shell in the center and fill with curry. Serve with rice, raita and pappadam. Garnish with chervil.

Serves 6.

CULINARY NOTES:

How to peel ginger: If you use a knife to remove the skin from a piece of ginger you will find that a good portion of the ginger root comes off with the skin. Try using a spoon to scrape the skin away from the root. The skin is very thin and will come away with a few scrapes. You will also be able to use the tip of the spoon to get into all the little cracks and crevices.

Designed to recognize creativity aboard the world's leading cruise and ferry lines, the BACARDI® Cruise Competition calls for bartenders and chefs to create recipes incorporating and drawing inspiration from BACARDI® products.

Cruise line bartenders and chefs from twenty-two cruise and ferry lines are invited to create inspired new cocktails and culinary recipes using world-class products such as BACARDI® rums and BOMBAY SAPPHIRE® gin, to name only a few as well as liqueurs like DRAMBUIE® and DISARONNO®.

Recipes are judged by Johnson & Wales University, the Show Tenders and a VIP panel comprised of cruise line executives, culinary experts, cocktail specialists and press. The highest rated cocktail and culinary recipes are awarded the Bacardi Bartender of the Year and Bacardi Chef of the Year honors as well as a cash scholarship for independent study.

For the past five years, Royal Caribbean International has taken part and won in the BACARDI® "Bartender & Chef" Cruise Competition creating mouth-watering recipes such as the ones presented in this chapter.

BACARDI.

SAUCE

2 tablespoons (30 g) butter
2 shallots, finely chopped
1/2 cup (120 ml) Martini & Rossi® dry vermouth
1/2 cup (120 ml) white wine
1 cup (250 ml) fish stock (page 158)
10 threads saffron, soaked in 1/8 cup (30 ml)
of warm water
1 1/2 cups (350 ml) heavy cream
1/3 teaspoon (1 ml) Worcestershire sauce
Salt and freshly ground white pepper

PASTA

1 pound (450 g) dry tagliatelli pasta
1 teaspoon (5 ml) extra virgin olive oil

SEAFOOD

3 (6 to 7-ounce) (200 g) lobster tails
Salt and freshly ground white pepper
2 tablespoons (30 ml) extra virgin olive oil

1 tablespoon (15 ml) extra virgin olive oil
1 clove garlic, finely chopped
12 large size shrimp, peeled, deveined
and tails left on (size 16/20)
Juice of 1/2 lemon
Salt and freshly ground white pepper

12 sea scallops
Salt and freshly ground white pepper
1 tablespoon (15 ml) extra virgin olive oil

1 teaspoon (5 ml) extra virgin olive oil
1 clove garlic, finely chopped
1 shallot, finely chopped
1 cup (250 ml) dry white wine
2 dozen fresh mussels, scrubbed and rinsed
Salt and freshly ground black pepper

GARNISH

1/4 bunch chives, chopped
1 red chili pepper, deseeded and finely chopped

Guenther Bartschte,
Senior Executive Chef, CEC

Chef Guenther started his culinary career in 1984 training in various hotels and restaurants in Germany and Switzerland. He started working on cruise ships in 1991 for Crystal Cruises and roamed the high seas for a while before establishing himself in Munich working as an Executive Chef for the then famous restaurant "Mangostin Asia." His love of travel made him move to Russia, the Middle East and various countries in Europe delighting guests at the Sheraton Hotels with his culinary delicacies. Chef Guenther came back to the cruise industry in 2000 and has been with Royal Caribbean International since then. When not onboard, Chef Guenther likes skiing and traveling around the world visiting friends and family.

"TREASURES OF THE SEA" TAGLIATELLI

Preheat oven to 450°F or 230°C.

For sauce, in a small saucepan over medium heat, melt butter and sauté shallots for 3 minutes until translucent. Deglaze with Martini & Rossi®; add wine and fish stock and simmer for 10 minutes or until sauce is reduced by half. Add saffron threads, cream and Worcestershire sauce, adjust seasoning with salt and pepper and simmer for 10 minutes or until sauce is thick enough to coat the back of a spoon. Do not boil. Keep warm.

Cook pasta in a stockpot of boiling salted water until al dente, about 8 to 10 minutes. Drain well and toss with olive oil.

With a sharp knife, cut lobster tail shells down the soft underside to expose the flesh. Devein and partially lift meat from shell. Season with salt and pepper and brush with olive oil. Broil lobsters in oven for 6 to 8 minutes until the tail meat is white. Keep warm.

In a sauté pan over high heat, warm oil and sauté garlic and shrimp for 5 to 7 minutes until shrimp are pink. Season with salt and pepper and finish with lemon juice. Set aside.

Pat dry and season scallops with salt and pepper. In a sauté pan, over medium heat, warm oil and sauté scallops, in batches, until firm and opaque, about 2 minutes on each side. Keep warm.

In a small stockpot, warm oil over medium heat and sauté garlic and shallots for 3 minutes, until translucent. Deglaze with wine, add mussels, cover and steam for 5 minutes or until mussels are open, shaking pot occasionally. Season with salt and pepper. Discard any mussels that do not open. Remove mussels from shells and set aside.

Add pasta to sauce. Toss to coat and serve in warmed deep plates. Arrange seafood on pasta and garnish with chopped chives and red chili pepper.

Serves 6.

GRILLED SCALLOPS AND ASPARAGUS RAGOÛT

Denis Schnitzler, Sous Chef

GARLIC CREAM
1 head garlic, peeled
1/4 cup (60 ml) vegetable oil
2 tablespoons (30 ml) heavy cream

RAGOÛT
1 tablespoon (15 ml) extra virgin olive oil
4-ounces (113 g) pancetta, diced
2 pounds green asparagus, peeled and diced

1/2 cup (120 ml) chicken stock (page 158)
Salt and freshly ground black pepper

SAUCE
1 teaspoon (5 ml) extra virgin olive oil
1 shallot, diced
1 tablespoon (15 g) tomato paste
3 tablespoons (45 ml) BACARDI® 8 Year Old Rum

1 cup (240 ml) chicken demi-glace (page 159)
1/4 cup (60 ml) heavy cream
Salt and freshly ground black pepper
1/4 cup (60 ml) milk

SCALLOPS
1 tablespoon (15 ml) vegetable oil
12 sea scallops
Salt and freshly ground black pepper

SALAD
2-ounces (60 g) arugula
2-ounces (60 g) frisée lettuce
2-ounces (60 g) lollo rosso
2 tablespoons (30 ml) truffle oil
8 green asparagus, peeled, blanched and cut in half
Salt and freshly ground black pepper

Preheat oven to 350°F or 175°C.

For garlic cream, in a small saucepan over medium heat, simmer garlic in oil for 5 minutes. Place garlic into a small baking sheet and bake for 10 minutes or until garlic turns golden. Transfer into a blender, add cream and mix well.

For ragoût, in a sauté pan over medium heat, warm oil and sauté pancetta for 5 minutes or until crispy. Add asparagus and sauté for 2 minutes. Add chicken

stock. Season with salt and pepper and simmer for 10 minutes or until asparagus are cooked.

To make the sauce, in a saucepan over medium heat, warm olive oil and sauté shallot for 3 minutes or until translucent. Add tomato paste and mix well. Deglaze with BACARDI® rum, add demi-glace, bring to a boil and simmer for 10 minutes or until sauce has reduced by half. Pass through a

fine sieve, add cream and garlic mixture and simmer for 5 minutes. Do not boil. Season with salt and black pepper.

Meanwhile, lightly oil a grill pan and heat over medium-high heat. Place scallops on grill and cook each side for 2 to 3 minutes, turning only once. Season with salt and pepper.

Keep warm until needed.

In a small sauce pan over medium heat,

warm 1/4 cup of sauce and mix with milk. Whisk well until foam forms.

In a stainless steel or glass bowl, toss lettuce and asparagus with truffle oil. Season with salt and pepper.

Place scallops atop asparagus ragoût. Finish each scallop with a spoonful of sauce and drizzle with foam.

Serve salad as a side dish.

Serves 4.

MARINATED SEARED TUNA AND SCALLOP TARTAR

Vairavan Ve, Executive Chef Administrator

LEMON SNOW
1/4 cup (60 ml) BACARDI® LIMÓN™ Flavored Rum
3 tablespoons (45 g) sugar
2 lemons, peeled and sliced thin

TUNA
2 tablespoons (30 ml) BACARDI® LIMÓN™ Flavored Rum
3 tablespoons (45 ml) extra virgin olive oil

1 lemon, peeled and thinly sliced
1/2 pound (250 g) tuna, skin off, trimmed into a roulade

1 teaspoon (5 ml) extra virgin olive oil (for searing)

SCALLOPS
2 tablespoons (30 ml) BACARDI® LIMÓN™ Flavored Rum

Juice of 1 lemon
2 tablespoons (30 g) chopped chives
1 tablespoon (15 g) chopped cilantro
8 sea scallops, diced

TOMATOES
4 plum tomatoes, peeled, seeded and cut into 1/2 –inch (1.2 cm) slices
3 tablespoons (45 ml) extra virgin olive oil
Salt and freshly ground black pepper

GARNISH
4-ounce (120 g) baby spinach
2-ounce (60 g) snow peas, blanched and cut lengthwise
Zest of 1 lemon
Chive sprigs

To make lemon snow, mix all ingredients into a small pan, bring to a boil and simmer for 5 minutes. Transfer into a stainless steel bowl and put in the freezer for 2 hours,

For tuna, mix all ingredients into a small stainless steel or glass bowl.

Pour marinade over tuna, cover and refrigerate for 1 hour.

For scallops, mix all ingredients in a small stainless steel or glass bowl. Add scallops to marinade, cover and refrigerate for 1/2 hour.

In a sauté pan over high heat, warm oil and sear tuna. Reduce heat and cook tuna for 6 minutes, turning occasionally. Tuna should remain red on the inside.

Transfer to a cutting board and cut into 1/2–inch (1.2 cm) thick slices.

Layer tuna slices in a circle on a chilled

plate. Using small pastry ring cutters, fill with tomato quarters then marinated scallops. Gently press with a spoon and transfer in the center of tuna rings. Top with baby spinach bouquet, julienned snow peas and a spoonful of lemon snow. Garnish with lemon zest and chive sprigs.

Serves 4.

Desserts

BERRY COMPOTE

1 cup (250 g) blueberries
1 cup (250 g) blackberries, quartered
3 tablespoons (45 g) sugar substitute
1/2 teaspoon (2.5 g) lemon zest
2 tablespoons (30 ml) water

PUDDING

3 egg yolks
3 eggs
1/2 teaspoon (7.5 ml) vanilla extract
1/4 cup (60 G) sugar substitute
3 cup (710 ml) heavy cream

PASTRY SQUARES

*1 sheet puff pastry, store bought
and cut into 3-inch (7.6 cm) squares*
1 egg yolk, beaten with 1 teaspoon (5 ml) water

GARNISH

1/4 cup (60 g) blackberries
1/4 cup (60 g) raspberries
1/4 cup (60 g) blueberries
1/4 cup (60 g) strawberries, quartered
1/4 cup (60 ml) heavy cream, whipped

SUGAR-FREE VANILLA PUDDING

Preheat oven to 215°F or 101°C.

To make compote, mix all ingredients in a small saucepan and simmer for 5 minutes or until berries are ready to burst. Remove from heat, transfer into a stainless steel bowl, cover and refrigerate for 1 hour.

In a medium size stainless steel or glass bowl, mix egg yolks, eggs, vanilla and sugar substitute and slowly whisk in cream.

Set greased 7-ounce or 200 ml oven proof ramekins in a shallow baking pan or baking dish. Place a spoonful of berry compote at the bottom of each mold and gently fill out with cream mixture.

Bake for 25 minutes or until a skewer inserted in the cake comes out clean. Refrigerate for 3 hours before serving.

For coulis, place remaining compote into a food processor and blend until smooth. Strain and refrigerate.

Meanwhile, lay pastry squares on a baking sheet lined with parchment paper, brush with egg mixture and bake for 7 minutes at 400°F or 204°C.

Using chilled dessert plates, create a square with mixed berries and top with puff pastry. Dip ramekins into hot water for a few seconds to easily remove puddings from molds and delicately place atop pastry squares. Garnish with a dollop of whipped cream, a garnish of red currant and a spoonful of coulis.

Serves 6.

CRÈME BRÛLÉE

2 cups (450 ml) heavy cream
4 egg yolks
1/2 cup (100 g) sugar
1/2 ripe banana, puréed
1 shot Bailey's® Irish Cream

CARAMELIZED BANANAS

2 tablespoons (30 g) butter
2 tablespoons (30 g) sugar
6 small bananas

GARNISH

1/4 cup (60 g) brown sugar
6 Sugar moons (purchased)
1 cup (250 g) assorted berries
Mint leaves

BAILEY'S® BANANA BRÛLÉE

Preheat oven to 350°F or 180°C.

In a saucepan over medium heat, slowly bring cream to a boil.

In a mixing bowl, combine egg yolks and sugar and beat until mixture is lemon colored. Place over simmering water and beat until mixture has doubled in volume, about 10 minutes.

Remove from heat and keep whisking to cool it down.

Slowly stir hot cream and Bailey's® into egg mixture. Using a fine sieve, strain into a bowl set over ice to quickly chill the mixture. Add puréed banana and mix well.

Pour mixture into individual molds set in a shallow pan or baking dish. Pour water into the pan until it is half way up the sides of the molds and bake for 40 minutes.

To make bananas, melt butter and sugar in a small sauté pan over medium heat. Add bananas and caramelize on all sides for a total of 2 minutes. Do not brown.

Evenly sprinkle top with brown sugar and place under broiler or use a pastry blow torch to heat sugar until it turns brown and bubbles.

Let set for a few minutes, then garnish with caramelized banana, Sugar moons, berries and mint.

Serves 6.

CULINARY NOTES:

Set the crème brûlée molds in a shallow pan or baking dish and place in the oven. Then pour warm water around the molds. This avoids spilling water on the floor or into the custard when placing the pan in the oven.

The water surrounds the molds and creates a thermal "jacket" around the custard as it bakes. As the water heats, it keeps the custard at an even temperature and helps the custard set evenly.

MANGO COULIS

1 cup (250 g) peeled and diced mango
¹/4 cup (60 g) sugar
¹/4 cup (60 ml) water

CAKE

Cooking spray
1 sweet pastry sheet, store bought
3 eggs
1¹/2 cups (350 g) brown sugar
1¹/2 cups (355 ml) canola oil
2 cups (465 g) whole wheat flour
1 cup (235 g) hazelnut flour
1 teaspoon baking soda
5 Granny smith apples, peeled, cored and quartered

GLAZE

¹/4 cup apricot glaze or apricot jam
3 tablespoons (45 ml) water

LOW-FAT APPLE CAKE

Preheat oven to 355°F or 180°C.

For coulis, over medium heat, mix all ingredients in a small saucepan and simmer for 15 minutes. Transfer into a blender and blend until smooth. Strain and refrigerate.

Grease a square cake pan with cooking spray, sprinkle with flour, knocking out excess and set aside. Layer with sweet pastry sheet and cut off excess.

In a large stainless steel or glass bowl, mix eggs, sugar and oil. Sift together dry ingredients and slowly add to egg mixture. Whisk well and pour into prepared baking pan.

Top with quartered apples and bake for 1 hour or until or until a skewer inserted in the cake comes out clean.

Transfer cake on a pastry rack and let cool.

In a small glass bowl, mix apricot glaze and water and brush mixture over cake.

To serve, cut cake in equal pieces and arrange on chilled dessert plates. Garnish with your favorite fruits and a spoonful of mango coulis.

Serves 8.

CHOCA-CHINO TRILOGY

White Chocolate Mousse

WHITE CHOCOLATE MOUSSE
1/2 cup (100 g) white chocolate
3 tablespoons (45 g) butter
1/2 cup (120 ml) heavy cream

5 eggs, yolks and whites separated
1/2 cup (100 g) sugar
1 tablespoon (15 ml) Grand Marnier®

1 cup (250 ml) heavy cream, whipped

GARNISH
32 raspberries
8 chocolate triangles (purchased)
Orange zest

In a small saucepan over low heat, warm chocolate, butter and cream until chocolate has melted. Stir to combine and set aside.

In a small mixing bowl, beat egg yolks with 1/2 the sugar and Grand Marnier®; blanch using an electric mixer at high speed for about 5 minutes or until mixture is frothy.

Slowly incorporate to chocolate mixture.

In a mixing bowl, beat egg whites with an electric mixer on medium speed until frothy. Increase speed to high and gradually add sugar, beating eggs until they form soft peaks. Fold in chocolate mixture and whipped cream.

Cover and refrigerate for 24 hours.

To serve, using a soup spoon dipped in warm water, delicately scoop a spoonful of chocolate mousse and place atop chocolate triangle and raspberries.

Garnish with orange zest.

Serves 8.

Mud Cake

MUD CAKE ICING
1 pound (450 g) dark chocolate
2 cups (500 ml) heavy cream

MUD CAKE
1 pound (450 g) flour, sifted
1 1/4 pounds (570 g) sugar
1/4 teaspoon (1 g) salt
1/2 teaspoon (2 g) baking powder

1/2 teaspoon (2 g) baking soda
1/3 cup (90 g) cocoa powder
1 teaspoon (5 g) coffee powder
3 eggs
1 teaspoon (5 ml) vanilla extract
1/2 cup (120 ml) vegetable oil
1 1/2 cups (370 ml) sour cream
1 cup (250 ml) water

GARNISH
Apricot sauce (purchased)
Raspberry sauce (purchased)

Preheat oven to 400°F or 200°C.

In a small saucepan over low heat, warm chocolate and cream until chocolate has melted. Stir well and transfer into a stainless steel bowl; cover and refrigerate for 24 hours.

For mud cake, using an electric mixer at medium speed, mix all ingredients together for approximately 4 minutes. Transfer batter into a prepared 8-inch

(20.5 cm) cake pan. Bake for 35 minutes or until a skewer inserted in cake comes out clean.

Remove cake from oven and allow cooling to room temperature in pan. Transfer to a wire rack with a matching size sheet pan underneath and, with a serrated knife, slice off the middle top of the cake and spread the bottom with a fine coat (1/2-inch or 1 cm) of cold mud icing. Place top back on.

In a small saucepan over low heat, warm 1/2 of the remaining icing (the rest will be used to make the Kahlúa® cheesecake). Evenly spread over the cake top and sides. Refrigerate.

Cut cake into triangles. Drizzle sauces on plate and gently arrange chocolate triangle with the point facing up.

Serves 8.

Chocolate Kahlúa® Cheesecake

FILLING

1¼ pounds (570 g) cream cheese, room temperature

¼ cup (60 g) sugar

5 egg yolks

¾ cup (150 ml) sour cream

3 tablespoons (45 ml) Kahlúa®

Remaining mud cake icing

DARK CHOCOLATE CHANTILLY

¼ cup (60 ml) heavy cream

¼ cup (60 ml) dark chocolate sauce (purchased)

GARNISH

8 chocolate butterflies (purchased)

Preheat oven to 400°F or 200°C.

In a mixing bowl, mix cream cheese and sugar and beat at medium speed, occasionally scraping down the sides of the bowl until fully mixed. Switch speed to low and add egg yolks one at a time until fully mixed. Add sour cream, Kahlúa® and cold mud cake icing. Mix well. Pour mixture into prepared individual molds. Bake for 45 minutes or until edges are set and center is firm. Remove cheesecakes from oven and let cool. Cover with a plastic wrap and refrigerate for at least 2 hours.

In a small mixing bowl over high speed, beat heavy cream until it forms soft peaks. Fold in chocolate sauce and refrigerate.

Before serving, finish each Kahlúa® cheesecake by piping dark chocolate chantilly atop cakes in the form of a rosette and garnish with a chocolate butterfly.

Serves 8.

VANILLA SYRUP
1 pound (450 g) sugar
1 quart (1 L) water
3 vanilla pods, cut lengthwise

PINEAPPLE
2 golden pineapples
12 vanilla pods

GARNISH
$^1/_4$ cup (60 ml) whipped cream
Candied cherries, purchased

VANILLA ROASTED SWEET PINEAPPLE

Robert Mead, Corporate Pastry Chef

Chef Robert joined Royal Caribbean International in January 2005. Robert was born in Sydney, Australia. From an early age Robert was inspired by the sweet creations from his grandmother's kitchen. Robert went on to complete his training in a small patisserie, finishing "Most Outstanding Student" in his year. Upon completion of his training Robert started his own pastry adventure, taking him to all corners of the globe in search of perfect sweet endings. Robert has a keen interest in sports, along with a passion for travel. He enjoys artistic ventures in his spare time.

Preheat oven to 400°F or 200°C.

Prepare syrup by mixing all ingredients in a saucepan and boiling until sugar is melted.

With a sharp knife, slice pineapple in half lengthwise and then cut into quarters. Peel and cut out the core. Pass vanilla pods through the quarters with a large needle.

Poach pineapple quarters for 5 minutes in the syrup, then transfer to a baking sheet and roast for 15 minutes, until the pineapple quarters are nicely golden.

To serve, place quarter of pineapple on each plate and garnish with a dollop of whipped cream and a cherry.

Serves 8.

PUFF PASTRY

2 cups (465 g) all-purpose flour
1 (5 g) teaspoon salt
1/2 pound (250 g) unsalted butter,
cold, cut in large chunks
1/3 cup (90 ml) water

Or

2 sheets puff pastry, store bought

FILLING

1/2 pound (250 g) almond paste, purchased
3 green apples, peeled, cored and halved
2 tablespoons (30 g) sugar
1 teaspoon (5 g) cinnamon powder
1 egg yolk, beaten with 1 teaspoon (5 ml) water

CRÈME ANGLAISE

2 egg yolks
1/4 cup (60 g) sugar
1 cup (250 ml) milk
1 vanilla pod, split lengthwise

GARNISH

Powdered sugar

APPLE PARCELS

Preheat oven to 390°F or 200°C.

To make puff pastry, combine flour, salt and butter and gradually add enough water to hold the dough together.

Transfer dough on a lightly floured surface and roll into a rectangle shape of about 8 x 12-inches (20 x 30 cm).

Starting with the closest short end, fold dough into thirds as you would a letter. Rotate the dough so the open side is at your right. Repeat the same procedure once more.

Wrap dough in plastic wrap and chill for at least 1 hour.

Place dough on a lightly floured surface with the open side at your right. Roll dough into a rectangle as before. Bring the two short ends together to meet in the center of the dough, then fold the dough in half again toward you. Rotate a 1/4 turn, so the open side is again at your right. Repeat the same procedure once more.

Wrap the dough and chill again for at least 1 hour.

Place dough on a lightly floured surface with the open side at your right, roll into a rectangle and divide in two.

Place first half of puff pastry on a baking sheet lined with greased parchment paper, spread with almond paste, top with halved apples and sprinkle with sugar and cinnamon. Brush borders with egg mixture and place second pastry sheet atop the apple filling, lining up the edges and firmly pressing the sides with your fingers.

Brush the top with egg mixture and cut a few slits to allow steam to escape while cooking.

Bake for 20 minutes or until pastry is golden brown. Transfer on a wire rack and allow to cool.

Prepare crème anglaise by creaming egg yolks with sugar. Bring milk and vanilla pods to a boil and slowly stir into egg mixture. Gently simmer for about 10 minutes or until cream coats the back of a wooden spoon. Do not allow sauce to boil. Remove from heat, pour into a glass bowl and stir to cool. Discard vanilla pod, cover and refrigerate.

Serve parcel on a dessert plate garnished with crème anglaise and finish with a dusting of powdered sugar.

Serves 8.

CRUST

½ cup (120 g) unsalted butter, melted
1½ cups (350 g) Oreo® cookie crumbs

FILLING

2 pounds (900 g) cream cheese, softened
¾ cup (150 g) sugar
⅓ cup (90 g) flour
3 egg yolks
½ cup (120 ml) heavy cream

1 teaspoon (5 ml) vanilla extract
1 pound (450 g) Oreo® cookies, crushed

MERINGUE

3 egg whites
¼ cup (60 g) sugar

BERRY COMPOTE

1 cup (250 g) raspberries
1 cup (250 g) blackberries
1 cup (250 g) strawberries
½ cup (120 g) blueberries

⅓ cup (90 g) sugar
1 teaspoon (5 g) lemon zest
¼ cup (60 ml) water

GARNISH

Powdered sugar
Mint leaves
10 chocolate twigs (purchased)

OREO® CHEESECAKE

Preheat oven to 300°F or 150°C.

For crust, pour melted butter over Oreo® crumbs and mix. Strongly press mixture into the bottom of a cheesecake or springform cake pan in an even layer. Bake for 10 minutes.

To make filling, in a mixing bowl, mix cream cheese and sugar and beat at medium speed until smooth. Add flour and beat well, occasionally scraping down the sides of the bowl until fully incorporated. Add egg yolks and heavy cream. Beat until mixture is light and fluffy.

For meringue, using an electric mixer on medium speed, beat egg whites and a pinch of salt until eggs are frothy. Increase speed to high and gradually incorporate sugar, beating egg whites until they form soft peaks.

Fold egg white meringue into cream cheese filling and gently mix until the batter is light and airy. Fold in vanilla extract and Oreo® crumbs.

Pour mixture into cake pan. Bake for 1 hour 15 minutes or until edges are set and center is firm.

Remove cheesecake from oven and allow to cool. Cover with plastic wrap and refrigerate for at least 2 hours.

For berry compote, mix all ingredients in a small saucepan and simmer for 5 minutes or until berries are ready to burst. Remove from heat, transfer into a stainless steel bowl, cover and refrigerate for 2 hours.

Upon serving, sprinkle cheesecake slices with powdered sugar and garnish with a spoonful of berry compote, mint leaves and a chocolate stick.

Serves 10.

DOUGH
3/4 cup (150 g) all-purpose flour
Pinch of salt
1/2 cup (115 g) granulated sugar
1 teaspoon (5 g) ground cinnamon
1/2 cup (115 g) unsalted butter,
room temperature
2 eggs
1 teaspoon (5 ml) dark rum

FILLING
2 pounds (900 g) Granny Smith apples,
peeled, cored and quartered
4 egg whites
Pinch of salt
1/2 teaspoon (2.5 ml) freshly
squeezed lemon juice

7-ounces (200 g) powdered sugar
7-ounces (200 g) ground walnuts
1 teaspoon (5 g) ground cinnamon
1 teaspoon (5 ml) amaretto

ICING
1/2 teaspoon (2.5 g) gelatin,
dissolved in a little water
1 1/2 cups (355 ml) heavy cream
1 tablespoon (15 g) granulated sugar
1 teaspoon cinnamon powder

GARNISH
1/4 cup heavy cream, whipped
14 strawberries
Mint leaves

Stefan Brueggemann,
Corporate Pastry Chef

Born in Altena, West Germany, Chef Stefan completed apprenticeship in Konditor and is a graduate from the Berlin Hotel School. Developing his skills by working his way throughout Europe, the Middle East and Asia, his love for travel is what made him decide to start a career at sea working for various cruise lines before joining Royal Caribbean International in 2007. When not onboard, he enjoys spending his time with his 2 sons and his wife as well as visiting Indonesia, the beautiful country where he now resides. His hobby, besides cooking, is world history.

WALNUT APPLE TORTE

Preheat oven to 355°F or 180°C.

In a medium bowl, lightly stir together flour, salt, sugar and cinnamon. With a fork, mix butter into flour until the mixture resembles coarse crumbs. Add eggs and rum mixing lightly after each addition, until pastry begins to hold together. With your hands, shape pastry into a ball.

On a lightly floured surface, roll pastry in 1/8-inch thick circle about 2-inches larger all around the pie mold.

Gently roll pastry circle onto rolling pin. Transfer to pre-greased high cake mold and unroll. With a sharp knife, trim edges, pinch to form a high edge and make a decorative edge by pressing it with a fork.

Lay apples over the dough.

In a stainless steel or glass bowl mix egg whites, salt, lemon and icing sugar and whisk for 2 minutes or until fully mixed. Fold in walnuts, cinnamon and Amaretto.

Gently pour mixture over apples and bake for 45 minutes or until a skewer inserted in the torte comes out clean.

For icing, in a small stainless steel or glass bowl beat heavy cream with sugar and dissolved gelatin.

Transfer torte on a rack and let cool. Pour icing over torte and sprinkle with cinnamon.

Place torte slices onto chilled plates and garnish with a dollop of whipped cream topped with a strawberry and mint leaf.

Serves 14.

POACHED PEARS

1³/4 cups (400 g) sugar
1 quart (1 L) water
2 tablespoons (30 g) peeled, chopped ginger
6 pears, peeled and cored

1 tablespoon (15 g) butter
2 tablespoons (30 g) sugar

CHOCOLATE TRUFFLES

¹/2 cup (120 g) semisweet chocolate
¹/4 cup (60 g) unsweetened chocolate
5 egg yolks
¹/2 cup (120 g) sugar
¹/4 cup (60 g) finely chopped galangal
2 cups (450 g) heavy cream
1 tablespoon (15 g) unsalted butter

¹/4 cup (60 g) cocoa powder

CARAMEL LICHEES

1 cup (250 g) sugar
¹/4 cup (60 ml) water
¹/4 cup (60 ml) whiskey
1 mango, peeled and diced
1 (8-ounce) (240 g) can lichees

GARNISH
Mint leaves

ASIAN POACHED PEARS WITH CHOCOLATE TRUFFLES AND CARAMEL LICHEES

In a saucepan combine sugar, water and ginger and bring to a boil. Add pears and simmer for 8 minutes, or until pears are tender. Remove from heat, cover and refrigerate.

In a double boiler over hot water, melt chocolates.

In a mixing bowl, combine egg yolks and sugar and beat until the mixture is lemon colored. Fold in chocolate and stir in galangal.

In a stainless steel bowl, beat cream until it forms soft peaks. Fold into chocolate mixture.

With buttered hands, shape mixture into 1-inch (2.5 cm) balls. Place balls on a sheet pan lined with parchment paper and freeze for 1 hour. Roll each ball in cocoa powder and refrigerate until serving.

For caramel lichees, in a saucepan over low heat, melt sugar and water and simmer until golden. Remove from heat and whisk in the whiskey very slowly. Add the mango and lichees and place back on the stove, simmering for 5 minutes.

To finish pears, warm a sauté pan over medium heat and melt the butter. Sprinkle pears with sugar and sauté on all sides for 2 minutes until nicely golden.

Arrange pears on plates, top with a mint leaf and spoon some caramelized lichees around them. Place a couple truffles on the plate and serve immediately.

Serves 6.

Romeo Bueno, Corporate Pastry Chef

Chef Romeo joined Royal Caribbean International in 1981 as an Executive Pastry Chef and has served as a Pastry Supervisor with the company since 1995. Hailing from Manila, Philippines, Romeo completed his pastry apprenticeship, then commenced his career at The Manila Royal Hotel as an Assistant Pastry Cook. Romeo also served at the 5-star Makati Executive Centre Hotel as the Executive Pastry Chef. Chef Romeo began his quest for international experience with Disney Cruise Lines as an Executive Pastry Chef. Romeo makes his home with his wife Eleonor and children Nicolo and Nicaella in the town of Rizal, Cainta, Philippines.

SHORTBREAD CRUST

1 ½ cups (370 g) flour
¾ cup (150 g) sugar
3 tablespoons (45 g) cornstarch
1 pinch of salt
1 tablespoon (15 g) lemon zest
1 cup unsalted butter (1 ½ sticks or 250 g),
cut into ½-inch (1.2 cm) pieces

FILLING

1 (16-ounce) (500 g) can peaches,
drained and sliced
1 (16-ounce) (500 g) can apples, drained
and sliced
¼ cup (60 g) sugar
1 teaspoon (5 g) cinnamon powder
¼ cup (60 g) raisins

CRUMBLES

1 ½ cups (370 g) flour
1 cup (250 g) sugar
½ cup (120 g) unsalted butter,
room temperature
or
1 vanilla sponge cake mix, purchased, baked as
per recipe and crumbled

CRÈME ANGLAISE

2 egg yolks
¼ cup (60 g) sugar
1 cup (250 ml) milk
1 teaspoon (5 g) orange zest

ROASTED PEACHES

1 tablespoon (15 g) unsalted butter
1 tablespoon (15 g) sugar
5 fresh peaches, halved

GARNISH

Cinnamon powder
10 scoops vanilla ice cream
¼ cup (60 g) slivered almonds, toasted

APPLE-PEACH CRUMBLE

Preheat oven to 300°F or 150°C.

To make crust, place flour, sugar, cornstarch, salt and lemon zest into the bowl of a food processor fitted with a stainless steel blade. Pulse several times to combine ingredients then gradually drop in butter pieces one at a time. Dough will reach a slightly crumbly consistency.

Transfer mixture to buttered 13x9x2-inch (33x23x5cm) baking dish. With fingers, press mixture into the bottom of the dish to form an even layer of crust.

For filling, place all ingredients into a stainless steel bowl and mix lightly.

For crumbles, combine all ingredients and hand mix until crumbles form.

Pour fruit mixture into pan and top with crumbles. Bake for 30 minutes. Let cool at room temperature.

Prepare crème anglaise by creaming egg yolks with sugar. Bring milk and orange zest to a boil and slowly stir into egg mixture. Gently simmer for about 10 minutes or until cream coats the back of a wooden spoon. Do not allow sauce to boil. Remove from heat, pour into a bowl and stir to cool.

For roasted peaches, in a small sauté pan over medium heat, melt butter and sugar; add peaches and sauté for 2 minutes. Transfer into a greased cookie sheet and bake for 7 minutes or until peaches are tender to the touch. Let cool at room temperature.

Cut cake into individual portions. Place on chilled plates, spoon crème anglaise around and sprinkle with cinnamon powder.

Serve cake with a side dish of vanilla ice cream finished with toasted almonds and a roasted peach.

Serves 10.

CULINARY NOTES:

If the crème anglaise has overcooked and the texture is curdled, try whisking the sauce using a wire whisk first. If this doesn't work, transfer sauce into a bottle and shake well. The action will homogenize the sauce and may produce a smoother texture.

CRUST

1 1/2 cups flour
1/2 cup powdered sugar
3/4 cup (175 g) unsalted butter, softened

Or
1 sweet pastry sheet, store bought or pie dough

CAKE
1 vanilla pound cake mix, purchased

CRUMBLES

1 1/2 cups (370 g) all-purpose flour
1 cup (250 g) sugar
1/2 cup (120 g) unsalted butter,
room temperature

CURD
4 egg yolks
1 can (14-ounce) (396 g) condensed milk
1/2 cup fresh lemon juice
2 to 3 teaspoons grated lemon peel

STRAWBERRIES

3 tablespoons (45 g) sugar
1 tablespoon (15 ml) Grand Marnier®
Juice of half lemon
1 cup (235 g) strawberries, quartered

GARNISH
1/4 cup (60 ml) whipped cream
Zest of 1 lemon

LEMON CURD CAKE

Preheat oven to 350°F or 176°C.

Grease a 13x9x4-inch (33x22x10 cm) baking pan and set aside.

For crust, combine all ingredients in a large bowl of an electric mixer and mix on low speed until mixture is crumbly. Press mixture evenly into greased baking pan.

If using a sweet pastry sheet, layer greased baking pan with pastry sheet cutting off any excess.

Bake 20 minutes or until light brown; remove from oven.

For pound cake, prepare batter as per instructions on the package.

For crumbles, combine all ingredients into a glass bowl and mix until crumbles form.

Blend curd ingredients in a medium bowl; pour mixture evenly over warm baked crust. Top with cake batter and finish with crumbles.

Bake for 15 minutes or until a skewer inserted in the cake comes out clean.

While cake is baking, mix sugar, Grand Marnier® and lemon juice in a glass bowl. Add strawberries, cover and refrigerate.

Cool cake on a wire rack and cut in rectangles.

Place slices of cake on chilled dessert plates and garnish with a dollop of whipped cream. Sprinkle plates with lemon zests and serve with marinated berries on the side.

Serves 8.

SOUFFLÉ

1 1/4 cups (300 ml) milk
1/2 cup (120 g) sugar
5 tablespoons (100 g) unsalted butter
1/2 cup (120 g) all-purpose flour, sifted
6 egg yolks
Zest of half an orange
2 tablespoons (30 ml) Grand Marnier®

8 egg whites
1 pinch of salt
1/4 cup (60 g) sugar

CRÈME ANGLAISE

6 egg yolks
1/2 cup (120 g) sugar
2 1/2 cups (600 ml) milk
1 vanilla bean, split lengthwise or
1 teaspoon (5 ml) vanilla extract

GARNISH

1/4 cup (60 g) powdered sugar

GRAND MARNIER® SOUFFLÉ

Preheat oven to 375°F or 190°C.

Butter soufflé dishes or ramekins and dust with a little sugar. Tilt and tap out excess.

In a medium saucepan, combine milk and sugar and bring to a boil.

In a small saucepan, over medium heat, melt butter and slowly mix in flour. Then stir in milk mixture. Slowly cook over low temperature, until mixture pulls from the saucepan, about 10 minutes. Do not boil. Remove from heat and slowly add egg yolks, one at a time, then orange zest and Grand Marnier®. This cream can be made in advance and refrigerated.

In a mixing bowl, beat egg whites and pinch of salt with an electric mixer on medium speed until eggs are frothy. Increase speed to high and gradually add sugar, beating egg whites until they form soft peaks.

Spoon one-third of egg whites into the Grand Marnier® mixture and gently mix until the batter is lightened. Fold in remaining egg whites, taking care not to deflate them. Divide the mixture into the soufflé dishes.

Bake for about 20 minutes or until the soufflés have doubled in size and are nicely browned.

Prepare crème anglaise by creaming egg yolks with sugar. Bring milk and pre-cut vanilla bean to a boil, then slowly stir into egg mixture. Gently simmer for about 10 minutes or until cream coats the back of a wooden spoon. Do not allow sauce to boil. Take out vanilla bean. Remove from heat, pour into a bowl and stir for a minute or two to cool.

Dust the soufflés with powdered sugar and serve immediately with crème anglaise.

Serves 4.

CULINARY NOTES:

We have all seen the soufflé used as a comedy device in television sitcoms. Scenes of frustrated housewives removing a lovely, golden-brown masterpiece from the oven, only to have it collapse before her tear-filled eyes, have been around since the dawn of television.

The soufflé is not as challenging as many people think. It does take practice and you will need to work out the baking time based on your oven's temperature.

To perfect the technique, make a batch of a basic soufflé mix and bake a few "practice soufflés." You will be able to see how the egg mixture rises and to spot where your oven is either too hot or too cool. One step you do not want to overlook is dusting the inside of the soufflé dishes with sugar. The sugar will give the egg mixture something to grab on to as it rises up the side of the dish.

RASPBERRY MOUSSE

2 tablespoons (30 g) sugar
5 egg whites
Pinch of salt
1/2 tablespoon (10 g) gelatin powder
1 tablespoon (15 ml) warm water
1/3 cup (90 ml) red berry fruit purée or raspberry
Melba sauce, purchased
1 cup (250 ml) heavy cream, whipped

PASSION FRUIT MOUSSE

2 tablespoons (30 g) sugar
5 egg whites
Pinch of salt
1/2 tablespoon (10 g) gelatin powder
1 tablespoon (15 ml) warm water
1/3 cup (90 ml) passion fruit purée or
1/2 cup (120 ml) unsweetened passion fruit
juice reduced by half
1 cup (250 ml) heavy cream, whipped

RASPBERRY COULIS

1 cup (250 g) raspberries
1/4 cup (60 g) sugar
1/4 cup (60 ml) water

MANGO COULIS

1 cup (250 g) diced mango
1/4 cup (60 g) sugar
1/4 cup (60 ml) water

CAKE

1 vanilla sponge cake mix, purchased
and baked as per recipe

GLAZE

1/4 cup (60 ml) mirror glaze, purchased

GARNISH

10 chocolate crescents, purchased
10 chocolate cigarettes, purchased

PASSIONBERRY DUO

For berry mousse, in a small saucepan over low heat, cook sugar until it reaches 250°F or 120°C. Do not boil. In a mixing bowl, beat egg whites and a pinch of salt with an electric mixer on medium speed until eggs are frothy.

Increase speed to high and gradually add cooked sugar, beating egg whites until they form hard peaks.

Dissolve gelatin in water and mix with red berry purée. Gently fold fruit purée with egg white mixture, then whipped cream. Keep refrigerated while making the passion fruit mousse.

For passion fruit mousse, in a small saucepan over low heat, cook sugar until it reaches 250°F or 120°C. Do not boil. In a mixing bowl, beat egg whites and a pinch of salt with an electric mixer on medium speed until eggs are frothy.

Increase speed to high and gradually add cooked sugar, beating egg whites until they form hard peaks.

Dissolve gelatin in water and mix with passion fruit purée. Gently fold fruit purée with egg white mixture, then whipped cream. Refrigerate for 15 minutes before using.

For raspberry coulis, over medium heat, mix all ingredients in a small saucepan and simmer for 15 minutes. Transfer into a blender and blend until smooth. Strain and refrigerate.

For mango coulis, over medium heat, mix all ingredients in a small saucepan and simmer for 15 minutes. Transfer into a blender and blend until smooth. Strain and refrigerate.

Cut sponge cake into 1/4-inch (1/2 cm) layers. Using a cookie cutter, cut out 8 rounds of cake and place into the base of each mold or ramekins.

Pour berry mousse over cake, half way to the top and refrigerate for at least 1 hour. Once set, top with passion fruit mousse and refrigerate for another hour.

Glaze with mirror glaze and refrigerate for 1/2 hour.

Dip molds into hot water for a few seconds to easily remove cakes from molds.

Drizzle both coulis on chilled plates, arrange cake in the center and garnish with chocolate accents.

Serves 8.

CULINARY NOTES:

What is a passion fruit anyway? Passion fruit is native to Brazil and is so named because the early Spanish Missionaries thought the flower's complex structure and pattern reminded them of symbols associated with the passion of Christ. It was said that the flower contained the lashes received by Christ, the crown of thorns, the column, the five wounds and the three nails.

The fruit is about the size of an egg with red, yellow or purple-brown skin. It has an intense, tart flavor and is used as an additive in juices to enhance the aroma. Both fruit and juice can be found fresh in most supermarkets or ethnic food markets. It is also available canned or frozen.

CHICKEN STOCK

*5 pounds (2.25 kg) chicken bones, including feet and
neck, or 2 roasted chicken carcasses*
3 quarts (2.8 L) cold water
2 carrots, peeled and coarsely sliced
2 medium onions, coarsely chopped
2 stalks celery, coarsely chopped
1 leek, washed and cut into 1/2-inch (1.2 cm) chunks
2 cloves garlic, crushed
2 bay leaves
3 parsley sprigs
1/4 teaspoon (1.5 g) black peppercorns

Place chicken bones into a large pot and pour in
cold water to cover by 2-inches (5 cm). Bring to a
boil, regularly skimming off fat and froth that rise to
the surface.

Once water is boiling, add remaining ingredients,
reduce heat to low, cover and simmer for 2 1/2 to
3 hours, skimming occasionally.

Strain stock through a fine sieve lined with several
layers of cheesecloth and refrigerate, uncovered,
overnight.

Discard congealed layer of fat on the surface and
strain once again into small containers or ice
cube trays.

Use stock immediately or freeze it and use as needed.

Makes 2 1/2 quarts (2.4 L).

FISH STOCK

BOUQUET GARNI
3 sprigs parsley
3 celery leaves
1 sprig thyme
1/4 teaspoon (1.5 g) black peppercorns
1 bay leaf

STOCK
2 tablespoons (30 ml) extra virgin olive oil
*1 pound (450 g) fish bones and heads from any
saltwater fish, except salmon*
1 carrot, peeled and coarsely sliced
1 shallot, coarsely chopped
1 small onion, coarsely chopped
1 stalk celery, coarsely chopped
1 leek, washed and cut into 1/2-inch (1.2 cm) chunks
1 clove garlic, crushed
1/4 cup (60 ml) dry white wine
5 cups (1.2 L) cold water

Prepare bouquet garni by wrapping parsley, celery,
thyme, peppercorns and bay leaf inside a piece of
cheesecloth and tying it with kitchen string.

In a saucepan over medium heat, warm oil and
sauté fish bones and vegetables for 8 minutes. Add
wine and stir, scraping the bottom of the pan. Add
bouquet garni and enough water to completely cover
fish. Bring to a boil, regularly skimming off fat and
froth that rise to the surface. Reduce heat to low and
simmer for 30 minutes.

Strain stock through a fine sieve lined with several
layers of cheesecloth.

Use stock immediately or freeze it in small
containers and use as needed.

Makes 1 quart (950 ml).

VEGETABLE STOCK

2 tablespoons (30 ml) extra virgin olive oil
1 medium onion, coarsely chopped
1 leek, washed and cut into 1/2-inch (1.2 cm) chunks
1 stalk celery, coarsely chopped
1 turnip, peeled and coarsely chopped
2 carrots, peeled and coarsely chopped
2 tomatoes, peeled, seeded and chopped
1 clove garlic, crushed
3 sprigs parsley
1 sprig thyme
1 bay leaf
1/4 teaspoon (1.5 g) black peppercorns
5 cups (1.2 L) cold water

Heat oil in a stockpot over medium heat. Add
vegetables and sauté for 10 minutes. Do not brown.

Add enough water to completely cover the
vegetables. Reduce heat to low and simmer for 30
minutes.

Strain stock through a fine sieve lined with several
layers of cheesecloth.

Use immediately or freeze it into small containers
and use as needed.

Makes 1 quart (950 ml).

BEEF STOCK

4 pounds (1.8 kg) beef bones
1/2 pound (250 g) veal trimmings
1 onion, coarsely chopped
2 carrots, peeled and coarsely chopped
2 stalks celery, coarsely chopped
1 leek, washed and cut into 1/2-inch (1.2 cm) chunks
1 tablespoon (15 g) tomato paste
2 bay leaves
3 parsley sprigs
1/4 teaspoon (1.5 g) black peppercorns
2 1/2 quarts (2.4 L) cold water

Preheat oven to 400°F or 200°C.

Place beef bones, veal trimmings and onion in a roasting pan and roast uncovered for 1 hour or until bones are golden brown.

Transfer to a stockpot. Add remaining ingredients and pour in enough water to cover completely. Bring to a boil, uncovered, over medium heat. Reduce heat to low and simmer for 8 to 10 hours. Set aside and let cool.

Strain through a fine sieve lined with several layers of cheesecloth.

Use immediately or freeze it in small containers and use as needed.

Makes 2 quarts (1.8 L).

BROWN SAUCE

BOUQUET GARNI
3 sprigs parsley
3 celery leaves
1 sprig thyme
1/4 teaspoon (1.5 g) black peppercorns
1 bay leaf

SAUCE
4 tablespoons (60 g) unsalted butter
2 medium onions, diced
3 carrots, peeled and diced
3 stalks celery, diced
1/3 cup (90 g) all-purpose flour
3 tablespoons (45 g) tomato paste
4 cups (950 ml) beef stock
Salt and freshly ground black pepper

Prepare bouquet garni by wrapping parsley, celery, thyme, peppercorns and bay leaf inside a piece of cheesecloth and tying it with kitchen string.

In a medium saucepan over high heat, melt butter. Add onion, carrot and celery and sauté for 15 minutes until vegetables are turning golden brown.

Reduce heat to low and add flour, stirring continuously until flour turns brown. Add tomato paste and cook for another 2 minutes.

Gradually whisk in stock, add the bouquet garni and adjust seasoning with salt and pepper. Bring to a boil, regularly skimming off froth that rises to the surface. Simmer for about 45 minutes, until the sauce has reduced by half.

Strain through a fine sieve lined with several layers of cheesecloth.

Use immediately or freeze it in small containers and use as needed.

Makes 2 cups (500 ml).

DEMI-GLACE

1 cup (250 ml) brown sauce
1 cup (250 ml) beef stock
Salt and freshly ground black pepper

In a medium saucepan over medium heat, combine the stocks and simmer for about 30 minutes, until reduced by half.

Strain through a fine sieve lined with several layers of cheesecloth. Adjust seasoning with salt and pepper.

Use demi-glace immediately or freeze it in small containers and use as needed.

Makes 1 cup (250 ml).

Beverages

The story of the Mojito cocktail dates back to the sixteenth century when an infamous pirate, Captain Francis Drake, set his eye upon the wealthy city of Havana. He did not take any treasures but instead left something priceless, the Draque, a forerunner of the Mojito cocktail.

Originally, the cocktail was made by combining aguardiente, sugar, lime, and mint. It was not until the mid-nineteenth century that rum replaced aguardiente and the Draque evolved into the Mojito cocktail.

Mojito

3 Mint leaves	Muddle mint leaves and lime in a tall glass. Cover with Mojito mint mix and fill glass with ice. Add rum and stir.
4 Lime wedges	
1 oz. (3 cl) Mojito mint mix	
2 oz. (6 cl) White rum	Top off with club soda and garnish with fresh mint sprigs.
1 oz. (3 cl) Club soda	
Fresh mint sprigs	

Mango Mojito

2 Mint leaves	Muddle mint leaves and lime in a tall glass. Cover with Mojito syrup and fill glass with ice. Add rum and stir.
2 Lime wedges	
1 oz. (3 cl) Mojito syrup	
2 oz. (6 cl) Mango rum	Top off with club soda and garnish with fresh mint sprigs.
1 oz. (3 cl) Club soda	
Fresh mint sprigs	

Caipirinha

1¼ oz. (3.75 cl) Cachaça	Muddle all ingredients, pour into cocktail shaker filled with ice, shake over ice and pour into highball glass.
1 oz. (25 g) Sugar	
1 Lime, quartered	

Desert Pear Margarita

1¼ oz. (3.75 cl) Patrón Tequila	Fill shaker with ice and add all ingredients. Shake and pour in glass. Garnish with star fruit slices.
1 oz. (3 cl) Monin Desert Pear syrup	
½ oz. (1.5 cl) Triple Sec	
2 oz. (6 cl) Island Oasis® Margarita Mix	
1 Star Fruit	

Caribbean Cooler

1 1/2 oz. (4.5 cl) Coco Rum

1/2 oz. (1.5 cl) Triple Sec

1 1/2 oz. (4.5 cl) Orange juice

1/2 oz. (1.5 cl) Rose's® Lime Juice

1 oz. (3 cl) Sprite®

Orange peel

Fill cocktail shaker with ice. Pour all ingredients into the shaker except for the Sprite®. Spindle mix and pour into a poco grande glass.

Top off with Sprite® and garnish with an orange peel.

Golden Margarita

1 1/4 oz. (3.75 cl) Cuervo® Gold Tequila

3/4 oz. (2.25 cl) Cointreau®

3 oz. (9 cl) Margarita mix

Lime wedge

Combine all ingredients in a cocktail shaker with ice. Spindle mix and pour into a salt-rimmed margarita glass. Garnish with a lime wedge.

Frozen Mai Tai

2 oz. (6 cl) Pyrat XO Reserve rum

2 oz. (6 cl) Hurricane mix

2 oz. (6 cl) Passion fruit syrup

Pineapple slice

Maraschino cherry

Blend all ingredients with ice into a smooth consistency. Poor into poco grande glasses and garnish with a pineapple slice and a maraschino cherry.

Passion Colada

2 oz. (6 cl) 10 Cane rum

4 oz. (12 cl) Piña Colada mix

1/2 oz. (1.5 cl) Passion fruit syrup

Pineapple slice

Combine rum and piña colada into a blender. Add ice and blend until smooth.

Pour passion fruit syrup on the inside of a poco grande glass and gently fill with rum mixture. Garnish with a pineapple slice.

Non-Alcoholic Oreo® Cookie Cocktail

5 oz. (140 g) Vanilla ice cream

2 tablespoons (30 g) Crushed Oreo® Cookies

2 tablespoons (15 g) Chocolate syrup

Oreo® Cookie

Place ice cream and crushed cookies into a blender and mix until smooth.

Rim the inside of a poco grande glass with chocolate syrup and pour blended drink into the glass. Garnish with an Oreo® Cookie.

Long Island Iced Tea

1/2 oz. (1.5 cl) Vodka

1/2 oz. (1.5 cl) Bacardi® Silver rum

1/2 oz. (1.5 cl) Gin

1/2 oz. (1.5 cl) Triple Sec

2 oz. (6 cl) Sweet & Sour mix

Splash of Sprite®

Lemon wedge

Place all ingredients except Sprite® in a shaker. Add ice and shake well.

Pour into a pint glass and finish with a splash of Sprite®. Garnish with a lemon wedge.

Long Beach Iced Tea

1/2 oz. (1.5 cl) Vodka

1/2 oz. (1.5 cl) Cruzan estate light rum

1/2 oz. (1.5 cl) Gin

1/2 oz. (1.5 cl) Triple sec

2 oz. (6 cl) Sweet & Sour mix

1/2 oz. (1.5 cl) Cranberry juice

Splash of Sprite®

Lemon wedge

Place all ingredients except cranberry juice and Sprite® in a shaker. Add ice and shake well.

Pour into a pint glass and finish with cranberry juice and a splash of Sprite®. Garnish with a lemon wedge.

Sour Apple Martini

1 1/2 oz. (4.5 cl) Vodka

1/2 oz. (1.5 cl) Pucker sour apple

1/2 oz. (1.5 cl) Sweet and Sour mix

Fill a cocktail shaker with ice and pour all ingredients over. Shake and strain into a chilled Martini glass.

Perfect Rob Roy

2 oz. (6 cl) Dewar's scotch whisky

1/4 oz. (0.75 cl) Sweet vermouth

1/4 oz. (0.75 cl) Dry vermouth

Maraschino cherry

Fill a cocktail shaker with ice and pour all ingredients over. Shake and strain into a chilled Martini glass. Garnish with a maraschino cherry.

Coconut Martini

1 1/2 oz. (4.5 cl) Coconut rum

1/2 oz. (1.5 cl) DiSaronno Originale

1 oz. (3 cl) Pineapple juice

1/2 oz. Orange juice

Lemon twist

Fill a cocktail shaker with ice and pour all ingredients over. Shake and strain into a chilled Martini glass. Garnish with a lemon twist.

Pomegranate Cosmo

1 1/2 oz. (4.5 cl) Citron Vodka

1/2 oz. (1.5 cl) Pomegranate liqueur

1/2 oz. (1.5 cl) Pomegranate syrup

1 1/2 oz. (4.5 cl) Cranberry juice

Lime wedge

Fill a cocktail shaker with ice and pour all ingredients over. Shake and strain into a chilled Martini glass. Garnish with a lime wedge.

James Bond Martini

1 1/2 oz. (4.5 cl) Gin

1/2 oz. (1.5 cl) Vodka

1/2 oz. (1.5 cl) Patrón Citronage orange liqueur

1/4 oz. (0.75 cl) Dry vermouth

Lemon twist

Fill a cocktail shaker with ice and pour all ingredients over. Shake and strain into a chilled Martini glass. Garnish with a lemon twist.

Mudslide

¹/₄ oz. (0.75 cl) Kahlúa®

¹/₂ oz. (1.5 cl) Bailey's®
Irish Cream

¹/₄ oz. (0.75 cl) Vodka

1 oz. (3 cl) Milk

In a shot glass, pour each ingredient in order listed. Use the back of a spoon to carefully layer each ingredient on top of the other.

Banana Boat

¹/₄ oz. (0.75 cl) Kahlúa®

¹/₄ oz. (0.75 cl) Banana liqueur

¹/₄ oz. (0.75 cl) Tia Maria®

¹/₄ oz. (0.75 cl) Dark rum

In a shot glass, pour each ingredient in order listed. Use the back of a spoon to carefully layer each ingredient on top of the other.

Cappuccino

1 shot espresso

Steamed milk

Foam

Cinnamon

Pour a shot of espresso in a large coffee cup. Pour hot steamed milk on top of the espresso, filling the cup about 2/3 full. Add foam of the milk on top and top off with a sprinkle of cinnamon.

Captain's Call

1 oz. (3 cl) Kahlúa®

1/4 oz. (0.75 cl) Cognac

Freshly brewed coffee

Whipped cream

Chocolate shavings

Using a glass Irish coffee mug, pour the Kahlúa and Cognac in the glass. Top off with hot coffee and mound with whipped cream. Sprinkle chocolate shavings on top.

Royal Delight

1/2 oz. (1.5 cl) Grand Marnier®

1/2 oz. (1.5 cl) Bailey's® Irish Cream

1/2 oz. (1.5 cl) Tuaca® Liqueur

1 shot espresso

Pour all ingredients over ice into a cocktail shaker. Shake and strain into a chilled martini glass.

Cooking Terms

AL DENTE: Italian for "to the tooth" and is used to describe a food that is cooked until it gives a slight resistance when one bites into it.

BLANCHING: Cooking a food very briefly and partially in boiling water or hot fat as part of a combination cooking method. Usually used to loosen peels from vegetables and fruits.

BLENDING: A mixing method in which two or more ingredients are combined until they are evenly distributed; a spoon, rubber spatula, whisk or electric mixer with its paddle attachment can be used.

BOIL: To cook in water or other liquid at an approximate temperature of 212°F or 100°C at sea level.

BOUQUET GARNI: A blend of herbs and vegetables tied in a bundle with twine and used to flavor stocks, soups, sauces and stews.

BROIL: To cook by heat radiating from an overhead source.

CARAMELIZE: Fruits and vegetables with natural sugars can be caramelized by sautéing, roasting or grilling, giving them a sweet flavor and golden glaze.

CHIFFONADE: To slice into thin strips or shreds.

CLARIFIED BUTTER: Purified butterfat; the butter is melted and water and milk solids are removed: also known as drawn butter.

CONCASSÉ: To chop coarsely.

DEGLAZE: To swirl or stir a liquid like wine or stock in a pan to dissolve cooked food particles remaining on the bottom, using the mixture as the base for the sauce.

DEGREASE: To skim the fat from the top of a liquid.

DICE: To cut food into cubes.

DREDGE: To coat food with flour, breadcrumbs or cornmeal before frying.

FLAMBÉ: Pour warmed spirits such as brandy, whisky or rum over foods such as fruits or meat and then ignite it.

FOLD: To combine a light ingredient like egg whites with a much heavier mixture like whipped cream.

FRY: To cook in hot fat.

GELATIN: A colorless, odorless and flavorless mixture of proteins made from animal bones, connective tissues and certain algae; when dissolved in warm liquid it forms a jelly-like substance used as a thickener for desserts, cold soups and certain sauces.

GRILL: Cooking in which the heat source is located beneath the rack on which the food is placed.

JULIENNE: Foods cut into matchstick shapes.

MACERATE: Soaking fruits in liquid, such as brandy or other alcoholic ingredients, so they absorb that flavor. Macerate can also be fruits sprinkled with sugar, which draws out the natural juices of the fruit, creating a syrup.

MARINADE: A seasoned liquid in which raw foods are soaked or coated to absorb flavors and/or become tender before cooking.

MINCE: To cut or chop a food finely.

MONTER: To finish a sauce by swirling or whisking in butter until it is melted.

PAN-BROIL: To cook food uncovered and without fat.

PAN-FRY: To cook food in a moderate amount of hot fat, uncovered.

POACH: To gently cook food submerged in a simmering liquid.

PURÉE: To process food to achieve a smooth pulp.

REDUCE: To cook by simmering a liquid until the quantity decreases by evaporation.

REFRESH: The process of submerging food (usually vegetables) in cold water to cool it quickly and prevent further cooking.

SEAR: To brown a food quickly over high heat.

SEASON: Adding flavor to foods. Season can also mean to coat the surface of a new pot or pan with vegetable oil and placing in a hot oven for about 1 hour. As the oil burns off, the carbon residue fills in the small pits and grooves of the pan's surface making a smooth finish that helps prevent food from sticking.

SIMMER: To maintain the temperature of a liquid just below the boiling point.

STIR-FRY: To cook food over high heat with little fat while stirring constantly and briskly.

Index

Left to right: Josef Jungwirth, *Director, Culinary Operations*; Ken Taylor, *Director, Restaurant Operations*; Frank Weber, *Vice President, Food & Beverage Operations*; Corinne Lewis, *Manager, Catering & Retail Operations*; Bob Midyette, *Director, Beverage Operations*.

This cookbook is dedicated to the esteemed culinary professionals responsible
for creating the vast array of gourmet meals served in our dining rooms,
specialty restaurants and brasseries onboard.

*The discovery of a new dish does more for the happiness of
mankind than the discovery of a new star.*
Brillat – Savarin, 1838

Very Special Thanks to:

Our Chairman and CEO, Richard Fain; President, Adam Goldstein and Sr. VP Hotel Operations,
Lisa Bauer for their continued support of *Savor*ˢᵐ.

Additional Recognition to:

Corinne Lewis, Manager, Catering & Retail Operations and Cookbook Author who
organized, developed and coordinated the project; Josef Jungwirth, Director of Culinary
Operations, for his creative contributions; and Bob Midyette, Director of Beverage Operations
and Naomi Celaire-Hettema, Traveling Beverage Manager for their delectable libations.

Our Senior Chefs and Executive Chefs, for their dedication to culinary excellence.
The Hotel Directors, F&B Directors, Restaurant Managers, Beverage Managers and the
entire Food & Beverage and Service teams onboard, who make it all happen...24/7/365.

Our Food, Beverage and Service team shoreside.
Henry Lopez, Director Corporate Purchasing and his team and
Michelle Yanda, Manager Brand Innovation and Loyalty Marketing.

Our business partners: Chocolate à la Carte, Joseph's Pasta, Kansas Marine and the
dedicated Tad Ware & Company Publishing and Photography team for their creativity and support.

©2010 Royal Caribbean International

Printed in China